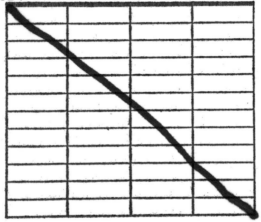

WHY TEACHERS ORGANIZED

WHY TEACHERS ORGANIZED

ORGANIZED

by Wayne J. Urban

Georgia State University

Wayne State University Press
Detroit, 1982

Library of Congress Cataloging in Publication Data

Urban, Wayne J.
    Why teachers organized.

    Bibliography: p.
    Includes index.
    1. Teachers' unions—United States—History. I. Title.
LB2844.53.U6U7 1982   331.88'113711'00973 82–
11160
ISBN 0–8143–1714–6

Chapter 4 of this volume was previously published in a
somewhat different form and is reprinted by permission of
the publisher from Diane Ravitch and Ronald Goodenow,
eds., *Educating an Urban People: The New York City
Experience* (New York: Teachers College Press. Copyright
© 1981 by Teachers College of Columbia University). All
rights reserved.

In memory of my mother, a teacher

Contents

Preface

This book attempts to answer the question of why teachers organized into workers' unions through a consideration of teachers' activities in a variety of circumstances and settings. Chapters 1 and 7 discuss teachers and their organizations as they reacted to administrative reforms in the 1890s and again between 1910 and 1930. Chapters 2 through 6 are case studies of teachers' organizational activities in three cities and in two national associations. The earliest such activity I describe began in 1897, when the Chicago Teachers' Federation was founded. Though teachers' associations existed in many cities before 1897, the groups which predated the CTF were primarily social organizations, presenting a marked contrast to the CTF, whose goal was to represent teachers' occupational interests. The latest organizational activity I discuss occurred in 1923, when Charles Stillman, a Chicago high-school teacher, resigned from the presidency of the American Federation of Teachers. Stillman, who had led the AFT since its founding in 1916, resigned a few years after the teachers' union had suffered a drastic loss in strength because of the successful membership campaign of its less militant rival, the National Education Association.

The years from 1897 to 1923, called by Richard Hofstadter the "age of reform," overlap to a large extent with the period commonly known as the Progressive Era.[1] These years marked a time of enormous change in many aspects of American life. Economic reformers sought to tame the trusts, those massive corporate concentrations of wealth which tried to control the marketplace; while in politics, particularly urban politics, reformers looked for ways to solve the excesses of boss or machine rule, which represented the undemocratic concentration of political power in the hands of a greedy few.

The public schools also underwent considerable alterations. By 1918, every state had passed a compulsory school law which necessitated a large increase in enrollment at all levels of the system. School boards had to accommodate a huge increase in students without greatly increasing the tax burden on citizens who had experienced a severe depression in the 1890s and faced the present and future with that experience firmly in their minds. Furthermore, increased enrollments meant more than a strain on the budget. The schools themselves became a prime arena for reformers who sought to reshape them to meet the demands created by new students and changed social conditions. School reformers sought alterations in governance, curriculum, teaching methods, teacher employment and retention policies, school buildings, and school administration.

This book, however, focuses primarily on schoolteachers and their organizations, not on school reform. Teachers' groups encountered reformers and their concerns on many occasions between the 1890s and 1920s, but as I argue after discussing several of these encounters, organized teachers usually were skeptical of reform because it threatened orderly employment and working conditions. I show that although at times teachers could and did ally themselves with reformers in coalitions which sought some particular change or group of changes, the two groups had different primary objectives. Teachers sought policies and procedures which would secure benefits and improve working conditions, while

10

reformers sought changes which would ameliorate some problem in the schools.

Coalitions like those between teachers and school reformers existed in several other areas of reform activity, and their prevalence, particularly in urban reform, has caused historians to rethink the entire reform phenomenon. While earlier studies sought to identify a particular group or orientation as typically progressive, more recent accounts have stressed that reform in the Progressive Era came as the result of shifting coalitions of interest groups, each pursuing its own goal through a particular reform or set of reforms. Teachers' organizations, when they joined these reform coalitions, acted basically as interest groups, and they followed their own priorities as they wound their way through the thicket of educational and political affairs. If their interests coincided with reform, they would be interested in reform. If their interests were not served by reform, they would oppose it.[2] The primacy of the organizational interest over reform concerns is illustrated in that both the greatest success and the ultimate failure of teachers' early organizational efforts occurred during and shortly after World War I, a period when reform had all but disappeared from American economic and political life. Teachers' organizations grew substantially in numbers and strength under the labor market stresses and dislocations caused by the war, and they suffered severe losses as a result of the wave of postwar conservatism.

In the course of preparing this study, I have found myself indebted to a variety of individuals and institutions. However, existing histories of teachers' organizations gave little specific information about just why teachers organized in the early twentieth century. William Eaton's history of the AFT and the works on the New York local union by Philip Taft and Celia Zitron stress the ideological debates which plagued the national and this local during the 1930s; there are no published book-length accounts of local organizations other than the New York unions. Several unpublished dissertations, however, proved helpful points of departure, as did published studies by David Tyack and Raymond Callahan which treat teachers' organizations as a part of larger educational topics.[3]

Geraldine Clifford of the University of California at Berkeley heard my initial attempt at this topic, a paper on the Atlanta teachers, in 1973. From that point on, she was unfailingly helpful in answering questions, reading drafts, and offering general encouragement. David Tyack of Stanford University, Paul Peterson of the University of Chicago, Paul Mattingly of New York University, and Joseph Newman of the University of South Alabama read the entire manuscript and offered helpful suggestions for improvement. Several colleagues at Georgia State University read parts of the manuscript and offered suggestions. In my own department, George Overholt and Edgar Gumbert deserve special thanks, as do Gary Fink and Merl Reed of the History Department.

My research on the Chicago Teachers' Federation was facilitated by two summers in residence at the University of Wisconsin. Herbert Kliebard, Carl Kaestle, Jurgen Herbst, and the late Edward Krug, along with several of their colleagues, helped the work along in many ways. I also benefited from visiting professorships at the University of Florida and the University of Alabama in Birmingham. Georgia State University generously granted a research leave for two quarters in the 1976–77 academic year.

I have never failed to find help from the librarians or archivists I encountered in pursuing this work. I would like specifically to thank Walter Bell of the Atlanta Public Schools, Jane Hobson of the Interlibrary Loan Division of Georgia State University, Archie Motley of the Chicago Historical Society, and Werner Pflug and his coworkers at The Archives of Labor and Urban Affairs, Wayne State University.

Two graduate students, Edward Buckner and Hilton Smith, read the manuscript at different stages and made helpful corrections. Pat Davis typed earlier versions of several chapters and the first draft of the manuscript. Lyn Eubanks and Anita Salamon typed the final draft. Jean Owen of the Wayne State University Press gave me a great deal of help in a brief initial interview, and Sherwyn Carr, also of Wayne State Press, was an extremely helpful and insightful editor who made the final stages of getting this book ready a pleasant and rewarding experience.

My family and I have had a running joke that I would acknowledge them by stating that without their efforts this book would have been finished two or three years earlier. They are here so acknowledged. Of course, I should also say that there is more to life than writing books, and my life would be unbearable without Judy, Leslie, and Bill.

Portions of this study were read in draft form at meetings of the American Educational Research Association and the History of Education Society. Part of chapter 1 appeared as "Organized Teachers and Educational Reform during the Progressive Era, 1890–1920," *History of Education Quarterly* 16 (Spring 1976): 35–52. A draft of chapter 4 was read at the 1978 Conference on Needs and Opportunities for the Study of Educational History in New York City, sponsored by the Institute of Philosophy and Politics of Education at Teachers College, Columbia University, and subsequently published as a chapter, "Teacher Organizations in New York City, 1905–1920," in Diane Ravitch and Ronald K. Goodenow, eds., *Educating an Urban People: The New York City Experience* (New York: Teachers College Press, 1981), pp. 187–218.

Abbreviations

AFL	American Federation of Labor
AFT	American Federation of Teachers
APSTA	Atlanta Public School Teachers' Association
CTF	Chicago Teachers' Federation
IAWT	Interborough Association of Women Teachers
NEA	National Education Association
NTA	National Teachers' Association
NTF	National Teachers' Federation

Introduction

In the late nineteenth and early twentieth centuries, public schools faced huge increases in enrollment. High-school enrollments, for example, rose from slightly under 200,000 in 1890 to almost 2 million by 1920.[1] In response, the number of teachers also grew. Two hundred thousand teachers were working in America's public schools in 1870; by 1900 the number had more than doubled. This increase continued between 1900 and 1920, but it was accompanied by a change which is important for understanding early teachers' organizations. Whereas in 1900 elementary-school teachers outnumbered secondary-school teachers by twenty to one, in 1920 that ratio had declined to six to one. Many of the new high-school teachers were men who commanded higher salaries than female teachers at any level. Because of this sex and salary difference, many early teachers' organizations, particularly those in the large cities, were differentiated according to sex and level taught.[2] Sex-based salary differences often presented a barrier to cooperation among these local organizations which could be exploited by board members, administrators, and other opponents of teachers' organizations to prevent the attainment of organizational objectives.

Despite the increase in the number of teachers throughout

15

the period, the age of most teachers remained relatively low, especially when compared to that age later in the twentieth century. The median age of a female teacher, which was twenty-six in 1900, had increased by only one year by 1920 and to twenty-nine by 1930, but it then leaped to forty-four by 1960. Even though they were relatively young, teachers between 1900 and 1920 taught for a median period of only five years before leaving the schools. Thus the picture of a young and inexperienced teaching force emerges clearly. In 1910, almost 8 percent of the male teachers and 11 percent of the female teachers were between the ages of sixteen and nineteen.[3]

Given their youthfulness, it is not surprising that teachers were also relatively uneducated. Throughout the period 1900 to 1920, the typical elementary-school teacher secured her position after some training in a normal school, an institution that offered work more akin to that of a high school than of a college. Secondary-school teachers resembled elementary-school teachers early in this period; in 1908, approximately half of the men and women teaching in the high schools did not possess a college degree. By 1930, however, secondary-school teachers had considerably widened the educational gap; 77 percent of them held a bachelor's degree, while only 12 percent of elementary-school teachers had attained that standard.[4] This difference in preparation, when added to the sex difference between the two levels of teachers, furthered the potential for a split between the groups' occupational interests.

Ethnically, few teachers came from recent immigrant families. In 1910, over three-fourths of the men and nearly the same proportion of the women were native-born English speakers. Within this larger pattern, however, there were some interesting deviations. According to a 1907 census report, native white women with one or more foreign-born parents were overrepresented as teachers compared to their percentage in the general population. In the larger cities, however, this was not the case; women having two native-born parents clearly predominated. The economic status of the families from which teachers were drawn was relatively low. In 1910, the average income of the family of origin of a male teacher was $639 and of a female teacher $813, figures which caused one student to describe teachers' families as subsisting on "little more than a bare living income." Teachers as a group, whether rural or urban, came from predominantly rural backgrounds; both male and female teachers were twice as likely to come from farm families as the population at large.[5] Thus teachers represented in microcosm the ongoing transition from farm to city that affected many aspects of American life during the Progressive Era.

Young, uneducated, rural, and poor teachers were not likely to exert a positive educational influence, according to one student of the situation. Lotus D. Coffman, a noted educator who received his doctorate for a 1911 Teachers College dissertation on the social backgrounds of teachers, concluded that the educational function of cultural transmission was being turned over to a group which was the least favored economically. The "intellectual possessions of the race are . . . left to a class of people who by social and economic station, as well as by training, are not eminently fitted for their transmission."[6] These views, widely disseminated and shared by other leading educators during the period, may well have widened the gap between working teachers and educational leaders which, as we will see, led to extensive changes in educational governance in the 1890s.

Coffman did point out some differences between urban and rural teachers which relate to the propensity of the former group to organize. In cities of over 25,000, 82 percent of the total teacher force was female, compared to 71 percent in towns and nonurban settings. In cities, both male and female teachers were more experienced than their rural colleagues. Urban males typically had taught for twelve years and urban females for seven years, while their rural counterparts, whether male or female, averaged only two years of experience. While over 75 percent of all rural teachers had five or fewer years of experience, only 29 percent of urban teachers were that inexperienced. On the other end of the scale, the same discrepancy existed; 11 percent of urban teachers had between sixteen and twenty years of teaching experience, while less than 3 percent of rural teachers were that seasoned. The median number of years of service for teachers in cities over 100,000 was ten.[7]

In 1910, one year before Coffman published his study, Carter Alexander published his own Teachers College doctoral dissertation on teachers' voluntary associations. Alexander's findings, when combined with Coffman's data, provide preliminary answers to the question of why teachers organized. Alexander made it clear early in his book that it was city teachers who made up the bulk of the membership of all teachers' associations, whether local, state, or national. Rural or small-town teachers usually did not join associations; if they did, it was almost always in response to pressure from their administrative superiors to join an administrator-dominated county association. City teachers joined groups which were usually both nominally and in reality independent of administrators. This difference meant, according to Alexander, that "city associations show a directness, and aggressiveness, and a persistence in promoting legislation of interest to their members which is seldom seen in any of the associations that cover larger areas." In these direct, aggressive city associations, women played an important role. Alexander noted that in over half of the thirty-one (out of forty-eight) cities of over 25,000 in which teachers' associations existed, there was an all female group. Moreover, he put his finger on the one significant reason why women formed their own organizations when he noted that they were not very influential in groups open to both sexes and all levels of school employees. He attributed this situation to the "traditional conceptions of women's inability to lead, the practice of assigning places in the associations to persons occupying certain [administrative] positions . . . and the lack of interest in the associations shown by most of the women members."

In contrast, the largely female city associations were made up mostly of elementary-school teachers who joined them to pursue the occupational objectives they shared with their peers, objectives which often separated their interests from those of their higher-paid high-school and administrative co-workers.[8]

Alexander described the most important general goal of city teachers' associations as "economic betterment." Teachers' salary woes stretched back at least fifteen years before 1910. In 1895 *Harper's Weekly* computed the national average teacher's salary at $260 per year, a figure it considered woefully inadequate. One year later, the *Atlantic Monthly* reported the dreadful economic and working conditions described by 1,189 teachers from throughout the country. The eminent psychologist, G. Stanley Hall, noted that these responses supplemented well-known statistics on the schools with "fresh confessions and first-hand observations and experiences from men and women actually engaged in school work." Hall cited the poignant story a Pennsylvania teacher told about the fate of one of his elderly colleagues: "In an adjoining town one of the occupants of the poorhouse is a man who had devoted a long life to teaching in the public schools of that county. Now old and infirm, he finds himself, through no fault of his, an object of charity." Hall also mentioned a Maine teacher's conclusion that "our best teachers leave for better salaries almost as soon as they have learned their work." Teachers were further plagued by onerously large classes, ranging from the lowest average of thirty-five per class in Maine to a high of fifty-eight per class in Montana. He added that classes were particularly large in city schools.[9]

When Hall's article was published in 1896, the plight of teachers might have been attributed to the economic depression afflicting the nation in the early 1890s. Teachers' salaries and other economic benefits, however, did not recover during the next ten years or fifteen years, despite a recovery in the economy. In 1911, Coffman concluded that teachers' salaries

19

were "very close to the bare minimum wage." It is therefore hardly surprising that in 1910 Alexander listed salaries as the first priority of city teachers' associations. Other specific economic objectives—hospital and burial benefits, pensions, and tenure—point to aspects of city teachers' search for materially secure careers in the public schools. Their formation of organizations for sickness and burial benefits had roots that reached back all the way to medieval guilds. This feature, present in most city teachers' organizations in 1910, predated the foundation of the city associations Alexander studied. He noted that in 1887, New York's teachers had formed a Mutual Benefit Association.[10]

For teachers it was a short, logical step from mutual aid to the pursuit of pensions. By 1910, many big-city associations had achieved local pension legislation and teachers had achieved a statewide pension system in New Jersey and Maryland. The Chicago Teachers' Federation, perhaps the most militant and certainly the most notable of the early teachers' organizations, grew out of the association Chicago's elementary teachers established in the 1890s to secure their recently won pension benefits. Pensions represented more than an old-age benefit. They were a step toward making teaching a genuine career. Coffman noted advocates' claims that pensions would "elevate the social status of teachers, raise their economic level, lengthen their term of service, encourage professional preparation, and raise the standard of certification"; this would lead to a teaching staff which would enjoy "greater permanency." Indeed, once teachers had secure pensions, they began to seek tenure to protect their claims to the economic fruits of a long career.[11]

In most cities, the pension and mutual fund issues were settled by 1910. The main goal of teachers' associations was a salary increase. Alexander remarked that "almost no cities . . . which have voluntary organizations of teachers, have failed to be the scene of organized effort . . . to better salaries," and he listed thirty-one cities in which salary drives had occurred between 1905 and 1910. In Philadelphia, for

20

example, the predominately female elementary-school teachers had organized themselves into the Philadelphia Teachers' Association in 1903. By June of that year, the association had enlisted practically every elementary-school teacher in its drive for better salaries, and it raised four thousand dollars to finance its efforts. It used this money to hold mass meetings of teachers, to secure signatures on petitions in favor of higher salaries from teachers and members of clubs and religious associations, and to sponsor visits from teachers in other cities who told of the salary gains they had achieved through organizational activity. The campaign was successful and, seven years after this success, the organization was still alive and continuing its pursuit of benefits.[12]

All of the teachers' organizations we will study, like the Philadelphia Teachers' Association, continued their battle for higher salaries and other benefits beyond any initial victory. Gains, once won, needed to be protected and improved upon. The salary scale was the best method of maintaining existing gains and improving the salary situation in the future. By 1910, a limited salary scale had been achieved in most cities, a welcome improvement for teachers who had previously been appointed yearly at any salary figure by their school board. Once a scale was achieved, city teachers' associations could seek to expand the number of steps on it, a goal which institutionalized experience as the most important criterion of competence for a teacher. However, the victory was far from complete. Coffman found that a positive correlation between salary and experience existed only in the first six years of teaching for men and for a slightly longer period for women. Thereafter, salary depended more on promotion to administrative position than it did on experience.[13]

City teachers' organizations fought hard both to maintain existing salary scales and to expand the number of steps; cost-conscious school boards, on the other hand, often sought to grant raises only to new teachers, thereby winning their allegiance and driving a wedge between them and their more experienced colleagues. The associations usually managed to defeat these initiatives and thereby to maintain the principle of experience, or seniority, as the major criterion of merit. While school boards might have to find more money to fund salary increases at all steps of the scale, this was balanced, according to Coffman, by the positive effects of the salary scale, the "advantage of encouraging the adoption of teaching as a permanent profession and of preventing frequent changes in the local teaching staff." [14]

My two major answers to the question of why teachers organized can now be formally stated. First, teachers organized to pursue material improvements, salaries, pensions, tenure, and other benefits and policies which helped raise teaching in the cities to the status of a career for the women who practiced it. Second, through the pursuit of salary scales and other policies, teachers sought to institutionalize experience, or seniority, as the criterion of success in teaching.

Teachers' devotion to seniority and their opposition to plans to curtail or abolish it lead to the conclusion that teachers' associations took a very traditional view of the occupational lives of their members. Despite their vigorous pursuit of material improvements, they usually were defensive in the face of reform initiatives which sought to change their working lives. Chapter 1 gives several glimpses of the confrontation between seniority-conscious teachers and reformers in the 1890s and early 1900s.

Chapters 2, 3, and 4 look at specific organizations in three cities, Atlanta, Chicago, and New York. The three cities, diverse in size and regional location, had teachers' organizations which reflected this diversity in their structures and programs. I will argue, however, that beneath this diversity was a more important similarity in goals and orientation. Chapter 2 describes the Atlanta Public School Teachers' Association, the group with the most uncomplicated goals and objectives of any of the local associations. The Atlanta group was almost strictly devoted to material improvements and was tactically quite conservative. In Chapter 3, I consider the Chicago Teachers' Federation, a larger group that was

22

led by Margaret Haley, a militant leader who often aroused controversy because of her vigorous pursuit of her organization's goals and her own desire for political reform. I argue that although Haley was different from those who led Atlanta's teachers, the members of each group were very similar. In chapter 4, I look at two organizations in New York City, one of which had a large membership of female elementary-school teachers, while the other consisted of a small, militant membership of male high-school teachers. I argue that the conservatism of the first group was much more appealing to most teachers, including those in Atlanta and Chicago, than the radicalism of the second organization. Thus the picture of the local teachers' association as conservative and materially oriented, developed in the Atlanta chapter, is modified but not discarded in the Chicago and New York chapters. This picture of a careful, cautious, benefits-conscious group of teachers may well be characteristic of teachers' groups in most other cities throughout this period.

Chapters 5 and 6 show how the occupational traditionalism and material orientation which characterized the successful local organizations also permeated teachers' efforts in two national organizations, the National Education Association and the American Federation of Teachers. The NEA's victory over the AFT, achieved in the early 1920s, is presented from the perspective of the leaders and members of each group. Chapter 5 on the NEA also shows how, for a time, teachers pursuing material benefits cooperated with administrators who had other objectives to take over the NEA from an aging leadership of university presidents and other lay people. The cooperation did not last, however, as the teachers' interest in material improvements and job protection collided with the administrators' drive for bureaucratic control of the NEA and the public schools. In the ensuing conflict within the NEA, the administrators emerged as clear victors.

Chapter 7 describes teacher-administrator conflict as it took place in several city systems between 1910 and 1930. Again, even organized teachers proved unable to defeat the

23

administrators' quest for bureaucratic control of the schools and the people who worked in them. In analyzing the administrators' victory, the structure and leadership patterns of teachers' associations prove significant. Teachers' leaders who bureaucratized their own associations were in a poor position to protect their members from the negative consequences of the bureaucratization of American education.

1

Teachers and the Corporate
Model of School Reform

Although teachers in several cities were attempting to organize themselves in the middle to late 1890s, their efforts were a minor eddy in the whirlpool of educational changes then taking place. The major issue for contemporary school reformers was the immersion of the city schools in city politics. School governance in most urban areas was vested in the hands of local or ward boards which administered the schools as simply another part of city government. Reformers decried this system as rife with potential and actual corruption. They charged that teaching jobs and other positions often went to friends or relatives of the ward board members or to the highest bidder, that textbook companies and other school contractors often paid board members in order to make sure that their products received favorable consideration, and that the ward trustees were on the lookout for themselves and their friends rather than interested in good education.

In 1896, the *Atlantic Monthly* published a series of articles on the schools which saw teachers' economic problems as susceptible to solution through reform of school management. Reform was needed not only to pay teachers large

25

enough salaries to live on, but also to give them security and the freedom to do their best work. The ward system clearly was the greatest impediment to that security and freedom. Reformers sought the same changes for school governance that were characteristic of advanced organization in business and industry. Large corporations were beginning to dominate American business life, and the pattern which they adopted, a small board of directors which made policy and a hierarchical administrative structure which implemented that policy, was recommended as the model for city schools. School boards should be small and centralized, representing the interests of good education rather than the desires and needs of local politicians, and the school superintendent, who typically had been a kind of secretary to the board and a troubleshooter in the system, should take on the duties of executive officer.[1] The corporate system of governance that reformers advocated, however, spoke indirectly at best to teachers' concerns. There is little evidence that teachers saw any connection between their own condition and that of workers in large industries, but ample evidence that teachers were wary of reformers' plans; they saw little relationship between governance reform and their own priorities. In fact, far from being strong advocates of reform, more often than not they opposed it. Analysis of New York teachers' opposition to reform in the 1890s serves as an initial step in understanding teachers and their organizations then and in the following two decades.

The relationship between administrative reformers and teachers in New York City was tense throughout the 1890s. In the late 1880s, the reformers were led by the noted philosopher and educator Nicholas Murray Butler, president of Teachers College and editor of the *Educational Review*. Butler and other reformers charged that the ward trustee system of school organization hampered changes in all aspects of school affairs because it put decision making in the hands of petty local politicians. The results were severely overcrowded classes averaging eighty-seven pupils per room, a curriculum that was "incomplete and disconnected," and teaching methods that were both rote and uniform. Butler believed that abolishing the ward trustee system was the key to achieving reform. The existing system was unnecessarily complex and graft-ridden, and the relationships of the ward or local boards to the central board of education were consciously unclear, meaning that responsibility for decisions on educational issues could not be attributed to anyone. This situation resulted in a stifling tendency to continue things as they were. Butler found the ward board's superiority over both the central board and the superintendent in personnel matters especially odious. The initiative in hiring rested with the ward trustees, a guarantee of political influence in the process and a likely indicator of a poorly equipped staff. Once a teacher was hired, dismissal for incompetence or even senility was next to impossible.[2]

Butler's answer to the situation was twofold: first, to put educational management in the hands of a board of school superintendents, professionally educated administrators who would control curriculum, supervise teaching, and decide on personnel practices; and second, to put overall control over school matters in the hands of a small, powerful central board of education, composed of businessmen and other men of affairs. Initially, the reformers were unsuccessful, beaten back by the political power of the ward trustees in the state legislature. In 1890 the central board failed to overcome ward opposition to Butler's plan to fill vacancies in high-enrollment wards with unemployed teachers from other wards. However, in the early 1890s exposés of educational conditions by Jacob Riis and Joseph Mayer Rice, both of whom highlighted the schools' problems as part of a larger indictment of urban political corruption, helped the Butler forces maintain their assault on the schools. As the ward trustees repeatedly defeated reformers' attempts to alter school management, Butler increasingly directed his attack on the trustees and their political control, rather than on specific educational deficiencies. By the mid-1890s, New Yorkers had become tired of the Tammany Hall machine which controlled city politics. In 1894 they elected a reform mayor, William L. Strong. Shortly thereafter, Butler was finally able to engineer a reform bill through the state legislature. It established a board of super-intendents and increased the power of the central board and the city superintendent while drastically limiting the powers of the ward boards.[3]

From the beginning of the reform campaign, teachers and other school employees were nearly unanimous in their op-position to it. Eleven different associations of school employ-ees helped the ward trustees defeat Butler's plan in 1891, and nine teachers' associations openly opposed reform in 1895. In the latter year, four thousand of the city's five thou-sand teachers heard the president of the Teachers' Associa-tion attack the plan for creating a board of superintendents and defend the efficiency of the ward boards of trustees.[4] In New York teachers were part of a large coalition opposing reform, one which contained nearly all school employees, most middle-class community and business leaders, most re-ligious leaders, and most political officials of both major par-ties. The ideology of this group emphasized local, ethnic, and religious loyalties, as may be illustrated in the following de-fense of the ward trustees by one central board member.

New York is a peculiar city. It is a cosmopolitan city. If you do away with the trustee system you do away with the people's schools. The trustees are in touch with the schools, and none others are or can be but those who live in the locality of the schools. We have a peculiar population, made up of all nationalities. They are people whose children we want to get in the public schools. There is a fear on the part of these people that we are going to interfere with their religion. If we have ward trustees representing all classes, confidence will be restored.[5]

Butler equated these localist sentiments with Tammany corruption, but the genuineness of reform opponents' alle-giance to their ethnicity, religion, and neighborhoods seems clear. They were willing to compromise and give some powers to a refurbished central board, such as a stronger role in managing the physical plant and in teacher licensing. They were adamant, however, on maintaining the role of the ward trustees in teacher hiring as well as in supervising school-community relations in order to protect the place of religion and other dominant community values in the schools. Similarly, a magazine which represented the position of the city's schoolteachers commented favorably on a reform which was then taking place in Brooklyn's schools (a separate system until consolidation of the city's boroughs in the late 1890s), noting that while the change strengthened the central board, it did not gut the valued role of the local trustees.[6]

There is considerable evidence that many teachers shared the community sentiments expressed by those opposed to reform; however, there were also more immediate reasons for teachers to object to the Butler plans. From the beginning of the reform campaign, Butler and his allies were openly critical of teachers. One of the reformers' loudest complaints was about the difficulty of firing incompetent teachers. Rice characterized the teaching in the New York schools as mechanical and dull. He attributed its weaknesses to the lack of any incentive for teachers to teach well, the absence of supervision which might lead to better teaching, and the cumbersome personnel policies which guaranteed a life tenure to teachers. Teachers were angered at the disdainful tone reformers exhibited in their discussions of school affairs. One school commentator noted the reformers' "brusque and arbitrary" treatment of teachers and warned, "In unfriendly hands the management of the teachers of the city would become as much of a machine as that of a body of mill employees."[7]

One specific reason that teachers opposed reform was the threat it posed to the orderly career pattern developed under the ward system. The problem lay not so much in the reformers' plan for a more powerful central board and weaker ward boards as in their proposal for a board of superintendents and a more powerful role for the city superintendent. Increasing the number of superintendents implicitly criticized both teachers and principals. Principalships, under the unreformed system of school administration, went to teachers on the basis of experience. Decreasing the importance of the principal by adding superintendents was thus a thrust at every teacher who was waiting her turn to become a principal.[8] One school paper called the proposal an idea of "a coterie of educational faddists, not one of whom has any personal knowledge of the New York schools." A better alternative, according to the paper, would be to make the principal "the immediate and responsible supervisor of the teacher." Strengthening the role of the three hundred principals appealed much more to teachers than adding a layer of supervisors at the superintendent level.[9]

In 1895, prior to the enactment of the Butler reforms, a dispute that erupted over a vacant primary principalship provides a vivid illustration of the seniority system teachers wished to protect and their arguments in its favor. In February of that year, a new principal was needed for the primary department of Grammar School 58. The departmental faculty reacted by nominating "Miss Egbert, our first assistant, [who] has been in the department for a long number of years, is imbued with the atmosphere, is acquainted with the necessary changes and their effects on the pupils—moving with the spirit of the times along approved lines, for she has taught, and has reached by merit the position she now holds." The ward board charged with making a recommendation to the central board ignored the faculty's nomination and chose instead another teacher, who was a low-seniority fifth assistant, not in a primary school, but in a male grammar department of another school. Grammar School 58's primary teachers objected on the grounds that the nomination "interfere[d] with the line of promotion, not only depriving [Egbert] of a merited position, but proving a manifest injustice to the other [teachers] in the department." In later argument over the issue, Egbert's supporters noted that she had thirty years of primary grades experience and that no allegations of misconduct had ever been entered about her work. They went on, "This being the case, and believing that the principle of regular promotion should prevail, we feel it is our duty to again ask at your hands favorable consideration for Miss Egbert's claim."[10]

After a four-month battle in which teachers defending orderly promotion induced the central board to reject three different nominees of the ward board, the ward trustees finally submitted Egbert's name and it was quickly approved.[11] This episode illustrates both the importance to the city's teachers of the seniority principle of promotion and the tenacity and ability they exhibited in defending it. Further, it indicates that the teachers, in defending the existing system, were not necessarily protecting a locally controlled ward system, but rather a system of divided authority between local and central board which teachers were able to manipulate to enforce promotions based on seniority. Teachers in most cities pursued salary scales to protect the same principle. In New York, reform threatened seniority in two ways. It withdrew personnel matters from boards which, as we have just seen, could be pressured to recognize seniority and placed these issues in the hands of a newly created board of superintendents whose actions could not be manipulated; and, by adding this new layer of superintendents, it reduced the fruits of the principalship.

One might wonder why teachers would not support the creation of more and more powerful supervisors in the expectation that the seniority system would simply add these posts at the top and award them to experienced principals as the positions became vacant. Reformers had made clear, however, that they had no intention of honoring seniority as a qualification for promotion. They preferred examination and education. If teachers and principals needed reminding that reformers did not value experience, they had only to look at neighboring Brooklyn, where an administrative reform similar to that proposed by Butler had greatly increased the number of superintendents and the power of the head

31

superintendent, William Maxwell, without benefiting teachers or principals. From their point of view, increasing Maxwell's power ignored the essential contributions of the principals and teachers to the Brooklyn schools, took parents away from the center of school affairs, and increased the potential for an educational one-man rule. Maxwell had never taught a public school class before assuming the superintendency and thus was irreparably handicapped by "that lack of intuition and practical insight, which can only come from a long and intimate association with public instruction."[12]

Butler had no more practical school experience than Maxwell. Their arrogance must have galled teachers and principals, even as in our time teachers chafe at critics who have no teaching experience. The ultimate victory of school reformers in New York meant that the old system of promotion by seniority was vulnerable to a group which would promote on the basis of education, examinations, and ratings by supervisors who had attained their own positions through the newer means. Thirty years later, a Chicago teachers' leader noted the unfairness of this system.

> There are in the elementary schools of Chicago today, men and women principals who never taught a day in an elementary school! On what basis of selection have they been placed over teachers who have years of experience in teaching children of elementary school age? Certainly they were not selected on the basis of demonstrated fitness to perform the function for which they have been set apart. There are in the Chicago schools today hundreds of experienced teachers supervised by principals whose sole claim to fitness for the position is that of having written an examination on academic subjects with particular emphasis on theory and method of teaching.[13]

Historians of administrative reform in the New York schools have proposed centralization of the school board and the concomitant loss of power by the war boards as the most important aspects of administrative reform. After looking closely at the teachers' opposition to reform, David Hammack concluded that teachers' antipathy to administrative centralization was based on both their occupational and community interests. He argued that teachers valued both the maintenance of their existing working conditions and the close relationship between themselves and parents and students that the ward trustee system provided.[14] My analysis leads to a different conclusion. In a situation like the dispute over the primary principalship of Grammar School 58, where occupational and community interests conflicted, teachers clearly chose the former over the latter. They aligned with the central board to block the ward board's attempt to interfere with the seniority-based promotion system. In terms of teachers' occupational interests, the key variable in reform in New York was not the change in board power from a local to a citywide base, but the addition of a group of superintendents who were expected to hire, promote, and dismiss on the grounds of education, examination, and supervisory rating, not seniority. Administrative reform meant a drastic change in teachers' career lives, a fact which was much more important than any community sentiments they shared with ward board members.

Reform plans for city school systems similar to the Butler plans for New York City were proposed and debated in several other educational forums in the 1890s. One of the most famous reforms took place in the Cleveland public schools early in the decade. In 1895, Andrew S. Draper, superintendent of Cleveland's schools when the reforms were implemented, recommended similar changes for other cities' schools in a speech at the National Education Association (NEA) convention. Basically, the Cleveland plan called for two revisions in school management: 1) a smaller, appointed board of education, with members chosen for their civic and business qualifications rather than elected to represent local or neighborhood interests; and 2) increased power over educational affairs for the superintendent and other central administrators. Both changes sought to reduce the graft and corruption which occurred when the schools were in the hands of a large, decentralized board of elected politicians.

According to the new plan, the superintendent, like a corporation president, was the man in charge, while the board had final control over general policy matters. Once the board made the larger decisions, it turned day-to-day control over to the central administrator. Draper's plan differed from Butler's in some particulars, but both attacked local control as corrupt and advocated a citywide board and a stronger superintendency, and the New York teachers opposed Draper as they had Butler. They noted that the Draper committee which proposed reform to the NEA contained only one member who had extensive teaching experience in public schools, making it similar in its ignorance of practical school affairs to the Butler group.[15]

Draper's plan did not go unchallenged on the floor of the NEA convention. Albert Bushnell Hart, a Harvard historian who had been a member of the NEA's famous Committee of Ten on secondary schools and was also a member of the Cambridge, Massachusetts, School Committee, raised several questions. He remarked that while he understood the rationale for altering board-member selection and increasing the superintendent's power, he was disturbed at two consequences of the changes. First of all, the provision to appoint rather than elect board members was undemocratic and certain to diminish popular interest in the schools. Hart argued that it ignored both the actual conditions and the traditions of localities and might even cause communities to abandon schools, since boards and managers would no longer be directly responsible to the citizenry. The second problem was that Draper's proposal totally ignored the role of teachers in school affairs. If teachers were to be better trained and screened, a Draper proposal which Hart accepted, then they ought to have a right of consultation on school affairs. Hart described the conception of teachers in the Draper plan as that of a "well run group of letter carriers." Instead he proposed, as a way to involve teachers in school administration, an idea which he had recently introduced in the Cambridge schools. He had asked teachers there to form an association

34

and elect representatives from it to a teachers' council. This body would be charged with considering the merit of various educational proposals, evaluating the proposals from the teachers' point of view, and recommending appropriate action to the authorities.[16]

Draper responded from the speaker's platform to both of Hart's objections. He did not agree that public support would be eroded by the reforms, though he offered no specific arguments to support his contention. On the teacher issue, he was more loquacious—almost combative. Draper believed neither a teachers' association nor a council were necessary if the reform plan were adopted. Reform meant that a powerful superintendent would be in a position to use the wisdom of the teaching force. Hart's desire to institutionalize the teachers' voice was unwise, because it would dangerously challenge the superintendent's authority. Draper wondered if teachers could ever be expected to contribute to school reform, given that they had regularly opposed change since the battle between Horace Mann and the Boston grammar schoolmasters in the late 1840s. Neither the citizenry nor the teachers could substitute for the expert management which would be provided by the corporate model of an appointed board and a powerful superintendent. Draper described the genesis of the Cleveland plan in a way that clearly drew the battle lines between reformers on the one side and teachers and uninformed citizens on the other.

> Four or five men in the city of Cleveland who are men of affairs— not teachers but simply business men—came together to reform this city school system; and they did not have the proceedings of the National Education Association, either, for a guide. They studied principles, and I think they succeeded pretty well.[17]

The fate of Hart's own proposal in the city of Cambridge illustrates further the tension between superintendents' claims to power in reformed administrations and the teachers' counterclaim to representation through their own organizations. Hart made his proposal for a teachers' association and council for Cambridge in 1894. The plan eventually was referred to a board committee in February 1895. During the next year, the school committee ignored it. Hart resigned from the committee early in 1896, thereby sealing the fate of teacher representation. The subcommittee which still had charge of his proposal finally reported in 1897, "it is inexpedient to take action." No reasons for the inexpediency were given in the board minutes, nor was any explanation published in the Cambridge newspapers.[18] The school committee, however, indicated a possible reason for rejecting the proposal when it adopted a new set of administrative regulations similar to the reforms advocated by both Draper and Butler. The Cambridge School Committee, alluding to increasing enrollment and the accompanying rise in administrative work, gave more power to the superintendent, reduced the number of subcommittees of the school committee, and limited school committee work to matters of "general supervision." Under the new rules, the superintendent nominated all teachers, took charge of all changes in the textbooks, and had "general authority over all educational matters." The school committee argued that these changes relieved committee members from time-consuming detailed administrative work and that they placed "more authority in the hands of the superintendent, thus concentrating responsibility and insuring expert management."[19] The committee's failure to provide a teachers' association indicated that in Cambridge, as in New York and Cleveland, there would be no place for an uncontrolled teacher voice in reformed school management.

Hart opposed administrative reform and advocated teachers' associations on different grounds than those of the New York teachers and principals. The Cambridge historian emphasized representative democracy and a kind of educated professionalism as the basis for his claims to a teachers' voice. He did not defend seniority and oppose the reformers' desire for education and examination in its place. Yet he did show, from a more disinterested perspective, that neither teachers nor ordinary citizens were of great concern to administrative reformers. The corporate model served the interests of those who proposed it: business and professional men and the school executives who would emulate corporation executives if reform were approved. The interests of teachers and ordinary people would be taken care of indirectly, if at all.

Educational reform, fueled by the publicity given to the activities of centralizers like Nicholas Murray Butler and Andrew S. Draper as well as by a general revulsion against urban political corruption, reached Chicago in 1898, when the mayor appointed a commission to study and recommend changes in school management. Within a year's time, the commission produced a report calling for changes in Chicago similar to those recently implemented in New York and Cleveland. Noting that the locally oriented existing board system dated back to a day when Chicago was a much smaller city, the commission proposed a smaller board, appointed on a citywide basis, which would have much less control over the daily affairs of the schools. Increased responsibility for educational matters, including curriculum, hiring, promotions, and dismissals, belonged in the superintendent's hands. The commission recommended a six-year term of office for the superintendent, a considerable increase in status and security over the former term of one year. It protected the executive from politically oriented dismissal by providing that termination could come only upon the presentation of written charges, which had to be approved by a two-thirds vote of the board.[20] Furthermore, the commission was not impressed by the city's teaching force. Noting that teachers had often been appointed by the board over the superintendent's objections, that they lacked any incentive to good performance, and that the existing system of salaries and promotions militated against improved teaching, it recommended a system of degree requirements, examinations, and increased supervision as a way of helping the superintendent improve hiring and promotions practices.[21]

The commission's report drew a quick response from a

37

coalition of labor, ethnic, religious, and school employee groups that was remarkably similar to the opposition to reform in New York. Opponents exposed the reformers' antilocalist bias and defended the principle of home rule in school affairs, under attack by reformers' attempts in 1899 (and in later years) to push their recommendations through the state legislature. Opponents characterized the increase in the superintendent's power as one-man rule, a drastic change from the democratic principles which were then operative in school management.[22] Some of the strongest arguments against reform came from the Chicago Teachers' Federation (CTF), a group organized in 1897 to protect the pension rights elementary teachers had won in 1895. The CTF differed from the New York teachers' organizations which opposed centralization. New York teachers, like most teachers throughout the country, had formed organizations primarily to serve their own social and self-improvement needs. The CTF, on the other hand, made clear from its inception that it sought improvements in salaries and other benefits and that it intended to pursue these goals with an activism not seen in any other teachers' groups.[23]

The CTF, like teachers in New York, had several reasons other than localist political sentiments to oppose the reform commission and its proposals. The commission chairman, the University of Chicago president William Rainey Harper, was no friend of organized teachers. In 1898, as a member of the Chicago school board, he had taken a leading role in denying teachers a promised salary increase, and the teachers and citizenry feared that the schools would become an employment center for graduates of Harper's university. Recommendations to increase the educational requirements for teachers were interpreted as both an attack on existing teachers and a dangerous extension of university power in school affairs. Harper's role in the dismissal of Superintendent Albert Lane, in the midst of the controversy over the commission's recommendations, further angered the city's teachers. At the prompting of the mayor, Lane, who had served the

38

schools for forty years, was summarily dismissed in favor of E. Benjamin Andrews, president of Brown University and one of Harper's close friends. Andrews brought to the city's schools a penchant for authoritarianism and a plan for consolidation, neither of which sat well with the teachers. The CTF, aided by local labor and women's groups, managed to defeat the reformers' recommendations in the state legislature in 1899.[24]

Despite their defeat, administrative reformers remained in control of the school board and the city government for the next few years and continued their attempts to alter school management. Superintendent Andrews resigned in 1900, citing political meddling in school affairs as his reason for leaving. In the next two years, the board moved to amend its own rules in ways that implemented some of the reformers' plans. The board gave the new superintendent, Edwin Cooley, a five-year instead of a one-year term of office, and it quickly adopted the new superintendent's plan for raises in experienced teachers' salaries. Under Cooley's proposals, teachers would receive raises, not according to their experience, but according to their "merit" as measured by examinations and supervisors' ratings. According to the board and the superintendent, this plan would reduce incompetence by rewarding teachers who performed well and not rewarding timeservers. The CTF bitterly opposed the plan, arguing that its conception of merit by examination and supervisory rating was abstract, unrealistic, and unrelated to the actual work of teachers. The examination provisions applied specifically to teachers with more than seven years' experience, a thrust at the older CTF members who had organized the federation to protect their pension rights. The CTF also believed that the merit system was a board-superintendent substitute for an across-the-board salary increase which had been promised since 1898 but had yet to be paid.[25]

The organized Chicago teachers, like New York's teachers, felt that true merit was grounded in seniority, experience. That principle had recently taken a blow from the state legislature when it struck the compulsory provision from the city's teacher pension law, making teacher participation voluntary and thereby effectively gutting the benefits. The superintendent's merit pay plan continued the assault on experienced teachers; frequent examinations were degrading to teachers whose competence was proved, in their own minds, by their years of service. Unsuccessful in persuading the board to oppose the merit plan, the CTF worked to replace the board by having its members elected, not appointed by the mayor. Teachers believed that the electorate shared their support for seniority and antipathy to the merit system. This effort also failed, but the CTF then turned its attention to electing a mayor favorable to their principles who might in turn appoint school-board members less enamored with merit and other administrative reform schemes. This effort proved partially successful when a new mayor, Edward F. Dunne, was elected with CTF backing and subsequently appointed board members who were more responsive to the teachers. The CTF used the opportunity to push through an alternative to examinations for establishing a teacher's merit, the completion of a course at the city normal school. This provision preserved the principle that experienced teachers were competent, needing at best to update their skills.[26]

The similarity in ideology and interests between administrative reformers and their opponents in New York and Chicago is striking. Teachers in both cities used local and community sentiments to buttress their arguments and defended seniority and experience against reformers who believed in formal qualifications and merit. The CTF noted the similarity explicitly, linking reform in Chicago to Nicholas Murray Butler and the centralization movement in New York City and charging that Butler was an elitist aristocrat with antiimmigrant, antidemocratic ideas. Robert L. Reid has aptly summarized the battle precipitated by the Harper reform recommendations as one "between the teachers who had organized in a quest for security and administrators who were seeking a clearer definition as to their own role in school management." This seems an adequate summary of events both in New York and Chicago if two points are added. Security meant to teachers the defense of their traditional employment and promotion patterns, while the administrators' clearer definition of their role in management meant an increase in their power over the teachers.[27]

Both reformers and their opponents used the term "professional" to support their positions. It seems clear, however, that the word meant something very different to the two sides. Teachers sought to preserve their existing employment conditions and therefore labeled attacks on them "unprofessional," while administrative reformers labeled their innovations attempts to "professionalize" the teaching force. In order fully to understand the conflict, one must have a specific conception of the professionalization process and of the relationship of each of these groups to it.

Most definitions of "professionalization" emphasize the importance of autonomy or job control by those who are "professional," as well as specialized training and intellectual techniques.[28] The reformers' desire, in both New York and Chicago, to gain control over school affairs for educated administrators seems much closer to the notion of professional autonomy than the teachers' goal of preventing that takeover. The teachers wanted to protect the already existing seniority system, and although they used it to ensure regular promotions (as demonstrated in New York) and to protect their regular salary increases (as in Chicago), ultimate control in this situation rested with lay people. This situation seems opposed to professionalism. Similarly, the administrators' desire for increased educational qualifications and examinations to determine merit seems closer to a notion of highly educated professionalism than the teachers' defense of experience as the major determiner of competence.

Teachers were protective and defensive; in seeking to preserve the status quo they resembled the shoemakers of Massachusetts in the mid-nineteenth century, who fought hard against the technological changes that transformed their work from a cottage to a factory industry. Or one might see in the teachers' behavior numerous analogies to the resistance to industrial capitalism that Herbert Gutman describes as typical of the behavior of several different groups of workers in the later nineteenth century. Administrative reformers attempted to begin in the schools a management system similar to the "new factory system" Daniel Nelson identifies as characteristic in private industry in the early twentieth century. Both the visibility of older, more experienced teachers in the opposition to reform and their defense of seniority as the major operative principle in their work life indicate that their ideology was much closer to that of the craft-oriented worker than that of a professional.[29]

The Chicago teachers' advocacy of councils similar to those proposed by Hart, on the other hand, might seem to contradict the characterization of teachers as not professional, since councils sought to locate influence over curriculum and other classroom matters among teachers who could claim to be knowledgeable about these matters. Hart compared the schools to the universities and sought the same power over educational matters for teachers that university professors enjoyed.[30] In Chicago, however, teachers' support for councils was not based on any principle, but rather reflected their allegiance to District Superintendent Ella Flagg Young, who had introduced councils in her district. Young had risen to the higher administrative level through the ranks, and as an administrator she consistently took proteacher positions. The Harper committee's call for councils throughout the city cited Hart's arguments and teachers' support of councils, but ignored the tie between teachers and Young's conception of administration. Thus, teachers opposed a reform package which they perceived as antiteacher despite its support of councils. Later on, when the board unilaterally implemented many of the Harper recommendations and sought legislative approval for the changes, teachers again objected, this time noting the absence of councils as one more indication of the autocracy that pervaded reform.[31]

In other words, teachers consistently opposed reform, whether with or without councils. Apparently their opposition to reform was much more significant than their occasional advocacy of councils. The teachers' fear of administrative power, their strong preference for experience over education and examination as a determiner of merit, and their devotion to democratic ideological arguments which supported lay control make them unlikely candidates for the label of "professionals" in the context of the centralization disputes. If any group was seeking autonomy and the institutionalization of rules which rewarded education and intellectual competence, cornerstones of professionalization, it was the administrative reformers, particularly the superintendents. Accounts of battles over centralization which emphasize localism or professionalism as important to the teachers' position cloud the crucial aspect of their arguments, their defense of traditional employment and promotion patterns. This defense should be kept in mind as we now turn our attention to teachers' pursuit of increased salaries and other benefits through the formation of their own associations in Atlanta, Chicago, and New York.

2

The Atlanta Public School
Teachers' Association, 1905–1919

At first glance, Atlanta, Georgia, may seem an odd place in which to begin a discussion of local teachers' associations. Its teachers' association was far less well known nationally than the Chicago or New York groups. Although the city was in the beginning stages of its recovery from the physical and economic devastation it had endured during and after the Civil War, it was still quite small in comparison to New York and Chicago. In 1902, Atlanta's population of 97,000 was about 5 percent of Chicago's almost 1.9 million and less than 3 percent of New York's almost 3.75 million. Like the rest of the South, the city of Atlanta had an ethnically more homogeneous white population than did the northeastern and midwestern cities, with their large numbers of immigrants. Atlanta's blacks were kept at a safe distance from whites through segregated schools and a segregated occupational structure. Atlanta's people, however, both black and white, were less concentrated geographically than the populations of New York and Chicago.[1]

Nevertheless, Atlanta aspired to become much more than what she was at the turn of the century. She saw herself as the capital of what Henry Grady, the editor of the *Atlanta*

Constitution, had proclaimed as the New South, a region which would abrogate its rural roots and take its rightful place in the prosperous business and industrial worlds of twentieth-century America. In pursuit of this goal, Atlantans could and did trumpet the economic growth taking place as the city and the region developed their natural and human resources. Atlanta grew at a phenomenal rate. In 1890, the city could claim 90,000 inhabitants, while thirty years later, it had more than doubled its population to over 200,000. It outdistanced both Chicago, which could claim only a 50 percent increase during the same period, and most of the southern cities which vied with it for regional leadership. Memphis, for example, grew by only 50 percent between 1900 and 1920; Atlanta, which had trailed it by 12,000 in population at the turn of the century, had surpassed it by almost 40,000 at the end of the second decade. School enrollment changes paralleled the population figures. Chicago's total enrollment of 225,000 in 1900 dwarfed Atlanta's 14,000. By 1920, however, Atlanta's student body had grown by over 100 percent, and Chicago's less than 50 percent. Despite Atlanta's superior growth rate, however, the numerical totals of both city and school populations continued to reflect the greatly different sizes of the two cities. In 1920 Chicago's 2.7 million people sent almost 328,000 pupils to public schools, Atlanta's 200,000 inhabitants enrolled 38,000.[2]

Atlanta's figures, however, were more representative of those of the average American city than the huge totals of Chicago or New York. Atlanta's single local teachers' association was more typical than the multiple organizations which existed in the twin metropolises of the Midwest and Northeast. In fact, the Atlanta teachers' reluctance formally to affiliate with labor and their hesitancy to link their own salary battles to political reforms like women's suffrage were representative of the caution which characterized teachers' associations in most cities. In his 1910 study of teachers' associations, Carter Alexander commented on the unwillingness of most teachers to embrace labor unions or take any other

45

actions which appeared dangerous, attributing their reluctance to "the necessity of keeping the public, which provides
the funds, favorably disposed."[3] In my analysis of local associations, I will argue that the attitudes of the Atlanta teachers were typical of most teachers, who, as we have already
seen, took a fundamentally defensive posture in New York
and Chicago when they were faced with threats to orderly
working conditions from administrative reformers. The Chicago labor militance and the political reform activity of teachers in both Chicago and New York were anomalies, for un-
derneath the apparent great differences between the Atlanta
teachers and their big-city colleagues was a significant similarity. All groups pursued salary and other material benefits
as vigorously as the local situation would allow. All groups
defended seniority. Differences in tactics were due more to
differences among the cities themselves and the leaders of
the respective associations than to any great differences in
the orientations of the teachers who made up the membership of each association.

Administrative reform came to Atlanta's schools in 1897,
just as it had come to New York and Chicago, but without the
same extended and bitter political battling and teachers' opposition. In 1897, the Atlanta school board was reduced from
seventeen to seven members at the behest, not of elite reformers, but of the city's elected politicians, the mayor and
the city council. These politicians used some arguments similar to those of reformers in the other two cities, but Atlanta's
elected officials were far more interested in controlling school
affairs through the new board system than they were in any
improvement in educational quality which would be achieved
by rewarding educational expertise. The mayor and councilmen, frustrated by the school board's unyielding defense of
corporal punishment in spite of considerable public opposition to it, dismissed the old board and replaced it with the
smaller board, comprised of one member for each of the city's
seven wards. The mayor also had other reasons to remove
the old board; he was particularly frustrated at the failure of

46

his recent attempts to involve himself in the board's hiring of teachers. Both the corporal punishment and the hiring issues suggest that in Atlanta reformers were attempting to repoliticize the schools, in contrast to those in New York and Chicago, who sought to remove the schools from the hands of politicians. The subsequent attention of the new Atlanta board members to the interests of their ward constituencies further illustrates the difference between reform in this city and in the other two.[4]

Another difference in Atlanta was the new board's more favorable attitude toward teachers. Shortly after taking office, the new board established four advisory faculties of the city's teaching force and enumerated their duties, using an argument that echoed the views of teachers' council advocates like A. B. Hart and Ella Flagg Young. "The policy of the Board has been to refer to these faculties important questions connected with the schools to the end that the teachers may feel themselves responsible not only for the management of the schools, after rules have been adopted, but also for the preparation of the best possible course of study, list of textbooks and general plan of control." Whether or not this move reconciled teachers to the change in administrative structure cannot be determined from contemporary documents, but it is clear that teachers played no vocal role in the brief flurry of opposition that did occur.[5]

The change in board membership did not go unnoticed or unchallenged in the city's press. The furor that greeted the move quickly died down, however, as the board moved to consolidate its position by simultaneously courting the politicians who had instituted the change and praising the old board members. Continuity in the superintendency in Atlanta, despite the change in board structure, may also help explain the absence of controversy. Though the new board attempted to give increased power to the Atlanta superintendent by giving him unprecedented rights—such as speaking in board meetings and asking him to keep the board informed on new currents in educational thought—Superintendent

William F. Slaton chose to ignore these opportunities and keep things as they were in the schools. Slaton, who had been superintendent since 1879, saw little need for change in the schools he already had headed for almost twenty years. He would continue in office for ten more years, retiring in 1907 at the age of seventy-six. He was succeeded in the superintendency by his son, William M. Slaton, who was as unimpressed by educational innovation as his father. The traditionalism of the Slatons blended nicely with the city council's desire to hold a tight rein on any increases in school funding. Board members' tendencies to push for large-scale and expensive innovations like manual training troubled councilmen, but the Slatons' suspicion of innovations helped councilmen to hold the line. The Slatons did not oppose educational improvement, but they saw it as coming mainly from increases in physical facilities, equipment, and teacher salaries, specifics which could be easily understood as desirable by both citizens and councilmen. The superintendents agreed with the politicians and citizens in dismissing most educational innovations as "fads and frills."[6]

The absence in Atlanta reform of increased power for the superintendent contrasts sharply with the New York and Chicago situations. Also missing was any threat to the teaching force through merit pay systems and other increases in supervisory power. Thus, though centralization came to Atlanta, it was not accompanied by alterations in political ideology or teachers' working conditions similar to those that characterized the changes in the other cities. This fact certainly seems to explain why the Atlanta changes provoked little lasting rancor among the citizens or teachers. We might conclude that the change in the board structure did not have any impact on the activities of the city's teachers, parents, and pupils.[7]

The traditional educational views of Atlanta's politicians and its superintendents blended nicely with those of the city's teaching force. Practically all of the teachers had been hired by one of the Slatons, and the superintendents' conservatism

48

constituted an implied vote of confidence in the teaching force in the same way that the new board's desire for change threatened it. However, the old board and the new board proved equally opposed to increases in salaries, which was a major goal of the city's school employees. As one of its last acts, the old board cut salaries in 1897. This action was repeated by the new board, which made a further salary cut one of its first actions in 1898. The city council, though an ally of the superintendent and teachers in opposing innovations, was not inclined to increase taxes for better teacher benefits. The council's continued unwillingness to raise more school revenue gradually brought the teachers, superintendent, and board together in a common campaign to pry money out of the council. In 1905, the teachers formed the Atlanta Public School Teachers' Association (APSTA) to facilitate their pursuit of higher salaries. Less than a year later, the board abetted the new association's salary drive by instituting a salary scale for school employees. The absence of any merit provision in the 1906 salary scale indicated that the board recognized the principle of seniority that reform boards fought in New York and Chicago; it was reaching a consensus on educational issues with the traditionally minded superintendent and the teaching force.[8] The institution of the salary scale marked the beginning of an era of cooperation among teachers, superintendent, and board that would continue until 1914. This cooperation was a marked contrast to the situations in New York and Chicago.

Operating within a traditional environment, both pedagogically and politically, the APSTA grew slowly. From the beginnings, it was firmly controlled by its senior members— principals, those who aspired to be principals, and high status high-school teachers. The association's program was narrow, confined to the pursuit of salary increases and other material benefits. As I have already noted, the teachers, and therefore their organization, tended to cooperate with school administrators and board members and thus one may say that the APSTA was structurally, tactically, and ideologically tradi-

49

tional. The APSTA's seemingly nontraditional actions—co-operation with organized labor in 1911, involvement in the opposition to educational reform between 1914 and 1918, and formal affiliation with the labor movement in 1919—can be seen to reaffirm the continuity of traditionalism.

From its very inception, the APSTA indicated clearly, through the leaders it selected, its method of conducting business, and its assent to the existing social and political environment, that it was not interested in challenging established ideas or authority. Early in November 1905, Dr. Theodore Toepel, a physician employed as director of physical culture of the Atlanta schools, met with Kate Massey and Lillie Wurm, both of whom were elementary-school principals, concerning the possibility of forming an association of the city's white teachers. Massey and Wurm were impressed with Toepel's proposal and agreed to pursue the subject. Other elementary-school principals were instructed to sound out their teachers on the idea, and at a late November meeting the principals reported that their teachers were greatly interested.[9]

The first meeting of the organization was held in December, with all white teachers, administrators, and the superintendent invited to attend. The membership elected Mrs. F. S. Whiteside president, Toepel vice-president, Nina Mitchell recording secretary, and W. F. Dykes treasurer. None of these officers was an elementary-school teacher, even though the great majority of the APSTA members taught in the grades. Whiteside and Mitchell were elementary-school principals, Toepel was a supervisor, and Dykes was a high-school teacher. Two of the four officers were males, though the school's teaching body was well over 90 percent female. This initial status and sex imbalance continued throughout the association's early years. Of thirty-four individuals elected to office between 1905 and 1919, three were supervisors, three were high-school administrators, ten were high-school teachers, fourteen were elementary-school principals, two were elementary-school assistant principals, and only two were elementary-school teachers. Approximately a third were men. The makeup of the board of directors, the legislative body of the association, was similar to that of the executive officers. Of forty-eight elementary-school directors, elected one per school in 1906 and 1910, twenty-one were principals or assistant principals, and sixteen were sixth- or seventh-grade teachers. These higher-grade teachers were next in line for principalships according to the schools' promotion system, which was similar to the New York seniority system. Obviously the APSTA hierarchy reflected the superiority of males and high-school teachers within the school system, while it also recognized the seniority principles of the system's regular employment and promotion pattern at the elementary level.[10]

The APSTA's existence as one single organization for all teachers contrasts with the situation in Chicago and New York, where elementary- and secondary-school teachers had separate groups, the latter usually being further divided along sex lines. The APSTA usually managed to avoid friction between elementary- and secondary-school teachers. There were only two high schools, one for boys and one for girls, as late as 1909, and only four high schools in 1920; there were not enough high-school teachers to form a separate group. Nor did there seem to be a need for separate high-school organizations, since the APSTA itself seemed to recognize and endorse, or at least did not dispute, the superiority in salary and status of high-school over elementary-school teachers.

As a general rule, the elementary-school teachers who made up the bulk of the association membership expressed little dissatisfaction with the APSTA leadership. Occasionally, however, critical questions were raised. In 1909, members proposed that the directors' actions be subject to approval by a two-thirds vote of the membership. The directors defeated this proposal, but later in the year they relented somewhat by allowing all matters of general interest to be submitted to the total membership. Carefully, however, they

51

pointed out that this concession was not to be construed as a surrender of their legislative power. Similar problems arose in 1916, when members unsuccessfully tried to open directors' meetings to the total membership, and in 1919 elementary-school teachers complained that a proposed new salary schedule favored administrators and high-school teachers.[11]

The dominance of administrators and high-status teachers suggests that the APSTA would be unlikely to take a combative attitude towards the school administration. This was precisely the case. On a number of occasions, the APSTA sought to enroll the superintendent as a member and invited school-board members to attend association meetings. In 1919, the superintendent was made an honorary member of the group. The association's official attitude was clearly expressed in a statement drafted in the 1920s, which read in part: "It must be true that Atlanta's comparative immunity from friction between the Board of Education and the Superintendent . . . and the principals and the teachers . . . has been in large measure a result of the cultivation of cordial relations and cooperation that the Teachers' Association has always fostered as a desirable condition under which to work and as essential to the success of the schools."[12]

One reason for cooperation between teachers, superintendent, and board, as I have already suggested, was their perception of a common enemy. The schools were statutorily the responsibility of the city council, which made all budgetary appropriations as well as many major policy decisions. It was not unusual for teachers, principals, superintendent, and board to agree on a proposal, only to have the council veto or refuse to fund it. Another explanation for the APSTA's cultivation of the superintendent and board was the political vulnerability of school employees, all of whom were elected annually to their positions by the board. The board, in turn, was appointed by the city council. Thus, in addition to the generally conservative Atlanta political climate, firm city council control of school finances and jobs mandated that the APSTA keep a tight rein on its members, lest some dangerous activity provoke a financial reprisal or the dismissal of the offenders or their leaders. The association's sensitivity to local politics is indicated by its choice of Mrs. F. S. Whiteside as its first president. She was a sister of Hoke Smith, a powerful Atlanta lawyer, former school-board member, and subsequently governor and senator from Georgia.[13]

The objectives of the APSTA were consistent throughout its first fifteen years of existence. When Toepel called for the formation of the organization, he voiced concern about salaries, class size, pensions, and job security. The association's original constitution called first for the improvement of teachers' salaries and working conditions, then for the promotion of their legitimate rights and interests, and finally for the cultivation of social intercourse among teachers. Of these three goals, the first was clearly most important. According to Mary Fant Gilmer, a member who wrote the early history of the APSTA, the association was formed "primarily to better the working conditions of Atlanta's teachers, and in this it bordered on a labor organization from the beginning."[14] From 1905 to 1919, the association devoted itself to pursuing higher salaries. Within a year of its founding, the APSTA sent a delegation to both the board of education and the city council to seek salary increases. Shortly afterwards, the board inaugurated a salary schedule for school employees, an event that implied support for the APSTA and the seniority system that pervaded the elementary schools. Once the schedule was implemented, the APSTA's chief goal was to gain increases for all those on the scale. In 1913, when the city council proposed a raise for elementary-school teachers only, the association objected and asked the council to include principals.[15]

When the APSTA sought an increase in salaries from the city council, it usually did so in conjunction with the superintendent and the board. Despite this careful cultivation of superiors, the results were often disappointing. Several times the board and superintendent would agree on a salary recommendation, only to see the council refuse to fund it or grant only a small portion. The council often gave increases to city employees such as firemen and policemen while withholding them from teachers. Teachers, the majority of whom were unfranchised females, could bring little effective pressure to bear on male council members. Councilmen held that women teachers did not support families, as policemen and firemen did, and thus did not merit the same treatment. In one case, when the superintendent attempted to counter this argument by collecting statistics on the number of teachers who were sole supporters of families, the council ignored the evidence, thereby further convincing those who believed that the teachers' main liability was their lack of the vote.[16]

Despite the council's frequent demonstration of the teachers' lack of political power, the APSTA chose against identification with individuals and arguments linking teachers' economic plight to women's suffrage. In 1911, one activist urged female teachers, who at the time comprised 400 of the 410 teachers in the Atlanta schools, to campaign for suffrage as the only sure way of receiving a salary increase. On another occasion, a suffragist attributed their economic deprivation to the "worm-like meekness of the great majority of teachers." She contrasted their timidity with the boldness of female factory workers, "poor ignorant women often with families dependent upon them [who] drop their work and walk out to return no more until conditions have been bettered." The APSTA turned a deaf ear to such appeals. When female high-school teachers waged an ultimately successful fight for equal pay with males between 1915 and 1920, they were forced to carry on their battle outside the APSTA, even though the *Journal of Labor*, the official newspaper of the Georgia labor movement, argued that it might eventually lead to equal pay for female elementary-school teachers also.[17]

The APSTA also avoided taking any position on educational policy. In 1907, when the issue of grading policies was brought before the group, it was dismissed without discussion. President Whiteside tabled a motion to consider raising the promotion mark in the schools as "inappropriate" for the organized teachers' consideration. The proper forum, she contended, was an advisory body of school administrators created by the board.[18]

It is evident, then, that the APSTA concentrated on economic issues and avoided both political reform and educational policy. This orientation, combined with the constant cultivation of the board and superintendent by those who led the teachers' association, suggests a strong desire on the part of all concerned that the APSTA remain noncontroversial. However, teachers' willingness to turn to organized labor for help in their 1911 salary fight thrust them for the first time into the midst of controversy.

At the beginning of the 1910–11 school year, teachers made a desperate plea for the salary increase that had been denied them since the adoption of the salary scale in 1906. They sought a scale which would range up from a minimum which was supposed to increase from $525 to $600 per year. This time the teachers altered their normally cautious methods. A new tone was apparent from the beginning of the salary drive. For the first time, salary proposals were stated as demands, not requests. The *Journal of Labor* responded as it had before, with an endorsement of the raise. The APSTA, however, in contrast with its earlier strategy of merely acknowledging labor's position, this time took the unprecedented step of sending a delegation to a Federation of Trades meeting to seek further help. The federation responded to the visit by authorizing a legislative committee to testify before the city council on behalf of the teachers and by inviting the teachers to send three fraternal delegates to labor meetings. The teachers also pressured recalcitrant councilmen by taking their case directly to the public. For the first time, they circulated petitions in favor of the salary increase, and the *Atlanta Journal* reported that thousands of signatures were obtained. The paper editorially endorsed the teachers' proposals.[19]

Despite this pressure, the city council responded only with

one-third of the total raise. This satisfied the board and the superintendent, but not the APSTA. At a mass meeting, the organized teachers dubbed the partial increase "hush money" and authorized an expenditure of five hundred dollars to hire a tax expert to investigate the city's tax structure and find the revenue needed to fund the full increase. It is quite likely that this action was patterned after that of Margaret Haley and the CTF, who in the early 1900s had successfully sued some of Chicago's large corporations for tax evasion.[20] APSTA willingness to take Chicago-style action in support of its pay demands was indicated in the original draft of the tax resolution, which charged that Atlanta's central business properties were undervalued for tax purposes. This explicit challenge to powerful business interests was softened, however, by removing the specific charges from the tax resolution before its final passage.

The teachers' meeting passed other resolutions which further indicated a shift toward more militant tactics. A committee of three was elected as a fraternal delegation to the labor federation, thereby reversing an earlier recommendation to investigate whether sending such representatives would "pledge the association in any way or indicate a friendly feeling."[21] Another result was a resolution deploring the statements of Councilman Asa G. Candler, who had called the teachers' association a "union of incompetents." The full council evidently shared his sentiments, since shortly after the teachers' meeting, in an obvious thrust at Theodore Toepel, it considered a resolution to abolish his job position of physical director of the schools. Council members "freely admitted that it looked mighty like a means of administering punishment to the esteemed doctor for running around trying to get the teachers to affiliate with the federation of trades and form a union."[22]

Toepel, obviously frightened by this last maneuver, was quoted in the *Atlanta Journal* as saying that the teachers' fight was finished. He indicated that the APSTA would bow to the wisdom of the council; it would neither hire the tax expert nor send the delegation to the labor federation. These views, however, proved not to represent those of the total membership. At a second mass meeting called to consider his statement, Toepel explained that it was his personal view and did not express the APSTA's official position, but this did not mollify the membership. It moved to follow the original course of action, hire a tax expert, and send the delegates.[23] For the first time, the leadership had lost control of the APSTA and it seemed headed toward militant political and economic action.

Cooler heads soon prevailed, however, and backed the APSTA away from its combative posture. The tax study, though completed, was never published. The fraternal delegation to the Federation of Trades, though sent, was never again mentioned in the association's minutes. By January 1912, a new APSTA president was urging "tactful dealings with men in high places" and the organization had abandoned its salary demands in favor of seeking smaller classes and more equipment. The city council's warning must have reached the rank-and-file as well as the leadership, since the total membership dropped over the next two years from 285 to 193.[24]

Even this brief and unsuccessful episode in militancy should not be taken as a total repudiation of the APSTA's traditionalism. Newspaper reports noted that while the teachers charged that business properties were undertaxed, their refusal to specify the names of individual tax evaders was another example of the association's being "altogether conservative and . . . careful not to go to extremes." The local labor federation, on the other hand, expressed shock and dismay at the council's repudiation of teachers' cooperation with labor as inappropriate, and the *Journal of Labor* remarked that "the federation of trades has always been conservative and reasonable and it still is." Trade unions did for workers what chambers of commerce did for businessmen;

the council thus had no more right to ignore the rights of wage earners, including teachers, to organize than it did to suppress business organizations.[25]

The APSTA's brief flirtation with mass militancy was thus in many ways an extension rather than a repudiation of its earlier policies. Nevertheless, the city council's antilabor reaction taught the teachers that even this small deviation in association policy was unacceptable. The teachers would remember the lesson for the next seven years, but the issue of labor affiliation was destined to reemerge, and with a different result.

In May 1918, a chain of events was initiated which ultimately led to the formal affiliation of the APSTA with both the Atlanta Federation of Trades and the American Federation of Teachers (AFT). It began with a controversy over the policies of the Atlanta school board under Robert J. Guinn, an administrative and pedagogical reformer who between 1914 and 1918 brought to Atlanta many reforms that had not been made in the late 1890s when the smaller board was introduced. Shortly after becoming a member of the school board, Guinn was elected president of it. He then served notice on school employees that he was seeking drastic alterations in school affairs by announcing his dissatisfaction with Superintendent William M. Slaton. Guinn was critical of Slaton's lack of interest in pedagogical innovations and his lack of initiative in administrative matters. The new board president wanted a superintendent with "stronger executive ability." Guinn's charges against Slaton were vigorously refuted by the *Journal of Labor* and two of Atlanta's daily newspapers, all of which endorsed Slaton's conservative educational philosophy and voiced suspicions of the changes Guinn favored.[26]

Slaton's supporters wanted to improve the schools through better salaries and physical facilities, a marked contrast to Guinn's call for wholesale pedagogical and administrative changes. They appealed to local sentiments in their defense of Superintendent Slaton, who, with his father, had controlled the schools for almost forty years. They criticized Guinn, who was not an Atlanta native, as an outsider who did not know or care about the real needs of the city's schools, and they buttressed their claim that Guinn's dissatisfaction with the schools had little popular support by collecting ten thousand signatures on petitions favoring retention of the superintendent. The APSTA, which might have been expected to back the superintendent, given his traditional philosophy and long experience in the schools, remained silent. One explanation for its inaction may well have been that teachers feared reprisals. The board showed that it was enamored with neither the APSTA nor the superintendent's defenders when it forced Theodore Toepel to leave the schools shortly after it dismissed Slaton.[27]

Guinn then served notice on the teachers and their association that he intended to alter school policies in ways that would financially penalize the teaching force. In 1915, the board adopted a merit system of pay similar to the one that Chicago's teachers had bitterly fought a decade earlier. Guinn indicated that a major reason for the new system was that it would reduce the payroll by approximately fifteen thousand dollars—most of which would come from reductions in the salaries of the high-seniority, high-salary teachers and administrators who were the backbone of the APSTA. Other innovations had similar results. When vacation (summer) schools were established, teachers found themselves having to work twelve instead of ten months, at a nominal increase in pay. When the Guinn board proposed to consolidate the city's high schools, it justified the change on educational grounds, while simultaneously arguing that it would save eighteen thousand dollars, two thousand of which would come from abolishing existing teaching positions. As he instituted these reforms, Guinn made clear that the teachers had no choice but to go along. One teacher wrote anonymously to the *Journal of Labor* in October 1915, objecting to the merit system as a device to cut salaries and to the growing tendency toward autocracy in the school board. She justified remaining anonymous by noting that "no teacher dares to express her opinion for fear of losing her position."[28]

In fact, teachers did not openly challenge Guinn until May 1918. At that time parents raised bitter opposition to Guinn's plan to consolidate the high schools. The nation was at war, and W. F. Dykes, the principal of Boys' High School, charged that the schools under Guinn had become pro-German. His accusation fanned citizens' passions to the point that the city council was forced to investigate the board's policies. Dykes, a member of the APSTA since its inception in 1905 and a frequent officeholder in it, noted in his testimony before the city council's investigating committee that the teachers' association was currently without a head because "it meant death in the front line trenches for a teacher to take a stand in regard to certain matters." Other APSTA members testified against the full range of reforms and criticized Guinn's autocratic and dictatorial relations with teachers. One teacher remarked that Guinn told his teachers that either they should get in "complete harmony" with his reforms or "get out" of the schools.[29]

The parents who testified against Guinn were some of the most powerful citizens of the city and this fact, combined with the anti-German political climate, forced both Guinn and his handpicked superintendent to resign. Complaining parents, organized into a School Improvement Association, joined with the influential *Atlanta Constitution*, the paper which had originally published the anti-Guinn charges, to follow up his resignation by advocating passage of a new city charter which changed the method by which Guinn had been selected as a board member. Instead of the old policy of appointment of board members by the city council, the new board members were to be elected by the populace. The APSTA watched hopefully as the charter amendment was considered. The amendment was approved, and teachers gained not only a buffer between the schools and the council, but also some financial stability. The new charter guaranteed the schools a set percentage of the city's tax revenue, independent of council approval.[30]

Given the demonstrated power of the School Improvement Association and the encouraging particulars of the charter change, the APSTA felt it safe to join forces with the charter reformers and work for the election of the School Improvement Association slate of board nominees in the November 1918 election. Victory followed, and the teachers attempted further to capitalize on their good fortune by announcing their desire for a 30 percent salary increase. It quickly became clear that there would be no increase, despite the recently guaranteed school income. A fall in property values during the preceding year meant that the expected increase in school revenue would not be forthcoming. Angry teachers responded by repeating their 1911 tactics. They held a mass meeting and called for an investigation of school finances; again they discussed the possibility of militant action. APSTA minutes report that a strike was discussed at the January mass meeting, but that it was deemed not appropriate at that time. Newspaper accounts, though they did not mention a strike, did indicate that something was amiss. "The spirit of the association has been conciliatory, but there are undercurrents which give evidence that the teachers are coming to a point where they would use more emphatic methods to obtain results."[31]

The mayor replied to the teachers by proposing that the city increase revenue by having the electorate approve a raise in the tax rate. The APSTA agreed to support the referendum only if it earmarked a specific portion of the increase for schools, and the mayor accepted this provision. The referendum was planned amidst newspaper reports that the spirit of the teachers was "cooperative toward board, council, and mayor." The voters, however, were not in the same spirit, and the tax increase was rejected, not once, but twice. Unwilling to rely totally on the mayor and the electorate, the APSTA resurrected another 1911 tactic, linking with labor. Affiliation with the AFT was considered initially at a February APSTA meeting, and it moved quickly to culmination after the defeats of the tax increase. On 12 May 1919, the APSTA officially joined the AFT, becoming Local 89. At the same meeting, the recently appointed superintendent, the W. F. Dykes who had sparked the Guinn investigation, announced a new salary scale which contained increases for all educators in the system.[32]

The negative political consequences of labor affiliation had diminished significantly since 1911. The change in the city charter had substantially reduced the city council's direct control over schools. The board, recently elected with association backing, voiced no objection to affiliation. The mayor, recently elected with union support, publicly approved affiliation. Superintendent Dykes signified his approval at the May meeting by sharing the platform with the unionists. Finally, the powerful *Atlanta Constitution*, a recent APSTA political ally in the Guinn affair, editorialized in favor of affiliation with the AFT. In short, teachers had successfully neutralized political opposition and embraced the union with the blessing of most of the city's political powers.[33]

A close look at some internal circumstances involved in the APSTA-AFT affiliation supports the argument that affiliation did not represent a repudiation of the APSTA's traditional structure and program. The AFT, formed in 1916, was engaged in a campaign to recruit new locals when it circularized the APSTA early in 1919, in the midst of that organization's salary battle. The Atlanta association's president authorized a committee of three members—one known to be for affiliation with labor, one known to be opposed, and one known to be neutral—to investigate affiliation and make a recommendation to the membership. The committee gathered more information on the AFT and presented it to the teachers at the April APSTA meeting, after which the members passed a motion asking the presidents of the AFT and the Atlanta Federation of Trades to address them at their May meeting.[34] At that time L. V. Lampson, the vice-president of the AFT, Atlanta Federation of Trades president Charles Gramling, and *Journal of Labor* editor Jerome Jones spoke to the teachers on the benefits of associating with labor. According to one member of the APSTA committee investigating affiliation, teachers opposed to unionization feared that they might be called upon to strike or support the strikes of other unionized workers. These fears seemed particularly real to teachers who could read in the Atlanta newspapers in 1918 and 1919 about strikes by street-railway workers, electrical workers, steam engineers, and railway clerks. Concerned teachers asked Lampson to explain the AFT policy on strikes. He replied that the AFT had an official no-strike policy and assured them that the union's alternatives of "political action, organization, and publicity" were more appropriate and productive for teachers. He did not have to mention that these were also basically the tactics that Atlanta's teachers had been following for fourteen years.[35]

Teachers' fears about the dangers of union affiliation were further allayed by trade unionists on the Technological High School faculty. One local federation of trades officer was appointed to it in the summer of 1919, joining there Ed Sutton, former president of the Atlanta Typographical Union and a former officer in the APSTA. Sutton, with thirty years of union experience, was chosen to rewrite the APSTA constitution before the affiliation. That constitution did not specify any change in the hierarchical structure of the teachers' association. Principals and other administrators were still eligible for membership.[36]

No doubt reassured by Lampson, Sutton, and the local labor leaders, teachers voted to affiliate with the AFT in May 1919. However, they did not vote at that time to affiliate with the local federation of trades, despite the presence of the local unionists and a pledge of support from forty-four Atlanta union locals to the teachers' association. The specific reasons for their reluctance are not clear. Some of their hesitancy may have been due to the relative immediacy of affiliation with local labor. Joining a national teachers' union would not have the same day-to-day impact on or consequences to teachers as linking up with organized workers in their own community. Another reason may have been labor's failure vigorously to support teachers in their 1918 fight against Robert Guinn. Organized labor had supported Mayor James L. Key, who was a Guinn ally in school affairs, and therefore had remained silent while the APSTA worked hard for Guinn's downfall.[37]

The local federation of trades nevertheless continued to support the APSTA throughout the rest of 1919. Jerome Jones told the city council in December that teachers "are near kinsmen of ours." Still, others grew impatient. In January 1920, one labor leader questioned the teachers' commitment, saying, "The school teachers of Atlanta owe much to the Atlanta Labor Movement and we are prone to ask ourselves the question at times, do they appreciate it?" Perhaps prodded by his statement, the APSTA affiliated with the Atlanta Federation of Trades in the same month. On 14 January, five delegates from the APSTA took their place at the meeting of the federation of trades. Ed Sutton gave the first teachers' union report to the local tradesmen, telling them that the teachers had been organized, not by the local labor unions nor by the national teachers' union, but "by the city council and the finance committee."[38]

Sutton's claim seems more accurate than perhaps he himself realized. Affiliation gave teachers one more weapon in their battle to secure economic improvement from the council. It did not alter the organizational structure of the traditional ideology of Atlanta's teachers. Their hesitancy in affiliating with the AFT, their concern over its strike policy, and their reluctance to embrace the local federation of trades all testify to the continuity of caution among the APSTA's members, even as they became unionists. The goals of the association remained primarily economic and the association's mode of operation was still hierarchical. The APSTA emerges as a hierarchically organized, traditionally oriented, pragmatic group which pursued one major goal—salary increases—and opposed administrative reforms that threatened teachers' salaries. Neither the organization nor the orientation changed when the Atlanta teachers formally affiliated with labor. This organization certainly seems different from the militant CTF and the politically radical New York City teachers' union, but before concluding that the differences among these three locals were significant, we must look closely at the other two.

3

Margaret Haley and the Chicago Teachers' Federation, 1897–1920

Margaret Haley was the most famous teachers' organization leader of the early twentieth century, known both to her contemporaries and to later historians of the teachers' movement as a fearless fighter for her cause. She led the CTF, the group representing Chicago's elementary-school teachers, into an unprecedented affiliation with organized labor in 1902, sought to persuade its members that women's suffrage and other political reforms were part of the teachers' cause, and personally confronted school administrators and the city's political and business leaders when they stood in the way of CTF goals. David Tyack, in his recent book on urban education, describes Haley by quoting the words of one of her contemporaries; she was a "lady labor slugger." Joan Smith, in a recent article on Haley and the CTF, has argued that the organization was a critical member of the coalition that pushed for political reform in Chicago in the early twentieth century.[1] This picture seems quite different from my account of the APSTA. However, the variance can be attributed to differences between Chicago and Atlanta and, even more importantly, to differences between Haley (and her coleader for much of the period, Catherine Goggin) and the leadership of the Atlanta teachers' organization.

Atlanta was a provincial city with a tightly drawn top-down power structure. Chicago was a brawling city, second largest in the nation and fifth largest in the world in 1890, with a much more heterogeneous population which included older Irish immigrants and many of the newer southern and eastern European immigrants who came to the New World at the turn of the century. Chicago's business elite could expect vigorous opposition to many of its programs from organized labor as well as from many social and political reform groups, which were often made up of "old stock" citizens who were threatened and angered by the economic superiority and cultural crudity of the new captains of industry. The business elite which sought to rule Atlanta and the rest of the New South had many ties to the Bourbons who had run the South after Reconstruction. Though political conflict was not absent in Atlanta, it was generally circumscribed by a larger consensus on political power which clearly defined the limits within which that conflict would be conducted, and Atlanta never experienced the progressive reform movement in politics and social life that pervaded cities in the Midwest and Northeast. Atlanta's labor movement also had less political influence and was less beset by internal disputes over reform issues than its Chicago counterpart. Atlanta's organized workers had never been blamed for a Haymarket Riot nor had they experienced the exhilaration of electing a reform governor who would pardon labor leaders arrested in connection with Haymarket and oppose the use of federal troops to put down a strike by workers of the Pullman railroad car company.

While Margaret Haley's personality and career clearly differed from those of the relatively unpublicized and generally timid leaders who ran the APSTA, we will see that there was a distinct similarity in the traditional beliefs of the teachers who made up the membership of both groups. Haley was often forced to channel her reform ideas to fit the less activist preferences and the economic interests of her members. The underlying tension between Haley and her constituents came infrequently to the surface; however, those infrequent occasions and Haley's own private views of her membership demonstrate that members lagged far behind her own advanced views on political and social issues. The CTF pursued salaries, pensions, and other material improvements, just as the Atlanta and most other local organizations did, but in Chicago the leaders espoused women's suffrage and other reforms, as well as affiliation with organized labor, as part of their pursuit of economic benefits.[2] Members were not as sure as their leaders of the efficacy of these reform efforts, although it is true that Haley and Goggin were able to alter the CTF structure in the late 1890s to enable them to pursue their reform goals, in tandem with the push for teacher welfare, with relatively little opposition. They instituted their own version of top-down leadership in the CTF, which members did not oppose as long as the leaders delivered economic benefits.

By the time Margaret Haley and Catherine Goggin assumed the leadership of the CTF in the late 1890s, they were veteran teachers with minimal formal training but a great deal of teaching experience, qualities they shared with the CTF membership and with the teachers who would form the backbone of organizations in other cities. Haley, born in Joliet, Illinois, in 1861, had completed grade and high schools by the age of sixteen; she then embarked on her teaching career, taking a position in an Illinois country school. After a year's teacher training at the state normal school in Bloomington, she began teaching in Chicago in 1883. She taught there from 1883 to 1900, and also completed one term of training at the Cook County Normal School. By the time the CTF was formed in 1897, Haley was an unmarried, thirty-six-year-old schoolteacher with fourteen years of experience in the Chicago schools. Goggin's background resembled Haley's, particularly in the amount of teaching experience. She began teaching in Chicago's elementary schools in 1872, immediately after her graduation from that city's Central

High School. Both of these leaders, as well as many CTF members, were Irish Catholics.[3]

The CTF had been organized around the major issue of teachers' pensions. Pensions were especially important for experienced, unmarried teachers like Haley and Goggin, who had made a lifetime personal commitment to the schools. They looked upon pensions as one way of assuring that that commitment would be properly rewarded. Teachers in Chicago began to seek pension benefits in the early 1890s, after the city granted them to the police and firemen. In 1895, the state legislature enacted a pension law for teachers, with benefits financed from a 1 percent assessment on each teacher's salary. The pensions quickly became controversial because of objections from high-school teachers who, though they contributed more to the fund than their lower-paid elementary-school colleagues, would receive the same retirement benefits. The fund also faced actuarial difficulties shortly after its enactment. The lax eligibility requirement made it easy for former teachers to return to teaching for a year and then become eligible for a pension, which immediately put pressure on the available funds. In the wake of these difficulties, the CTF was formed to protect both the integrity of the pension fund and the interests of elementary-school teachers in its continuance.[4]

Once teachers had won pensions, they recognized the need for job tenure. The school board officially recognized the importance of job security by providing that teachers could not be discharged except for cause, established by written charges and confirmed by a vote for dismissal by a majority of the board.[5] Tenure for Chicago's teachers thus reflected a pension-related interest in job protection rather than recognition of their right to academic freedom. While the two elements of tenure cannot be neatly separated, it is clear that from the beginning Chicago teachers were more concerned with job security than professional rights. This dominance of material interests would be reflected in many areas of CTF activity over the next two decades.

Pensions and tenure were not the only or even the most important goals in the CTF organizational program. Pensions had great appeal for older, experienced teachers, but a mass membership organization, which the CTF intended to be, needed an objective which would appeal to all elementary-school teachers. Margaret Haley identified that objective when she remarked that the CTF grew out of the needs of teachers, the "first and greatest thing being that of enough salary to live on." The salaries of Chicago's elementary-school teachers were particularly low. While high-school teachers and school administrators had seen their pay increase 14.5 percent in the twenty years preceding 1897, teachers in the lower grades had received only a 6 percent increase. The CTF's initial statement of purpose reflected this state of affairs, citing the attainment of the rights and benefits to which teachers were entitled as the objective of the organization, and listing an adequate salary as the first benefit.[6] In fact, the board of education acknowledged the plight of elementary-school teachers shortly after the CTF was founded, when it added two increments to the higher end of their salary scale. However, the board soon rescinded its action, claiming that a financial crisis had left the system without enough funds to pay the higher salaries. The CTF reacted quickly and vigorously, as it would do so often in later years. Apparently this aggressive pursuit of material benefits was attractive to teachers; CTF membership grew to 2,500 by the end of 1897 and shortly thereafter to 3,600, over half the total number of eligible teachers.[7]

The emphasis on salaries, pensions, and other benefits dominated federation activities throughout the early twentieth century. When the CTF sought support for a city charter revision in 1904, it appealed initially to the teachers by reminding them, "The Federation has always advocated the improvement of the material conditions of teachers, believing that such improvement lies at the base of all other aids to efficiency." Four years later, a CTF membership appeal was launched with an enumeration of the federation's past activities on salaries and pensions. In 1912, an appeal for dues payment was prefaced by a report of salary and pension gains. In 1913, a battle was fought to retain teachers' control of the pension fund and, one year later, the CTF restated its main priorities as protecting the pension and funding the existing salary scale. When a revenue shortage threatened salaries in 1915, the CTF fought board proposals to cut all salaries or eliminate the top two steps on the salary scale. In response to this latter proposal, the federation remarked that the last time those steps were eliminated, it took ten years to get them back. Nevertheless, unpleasant history repeated itself; this time it would be three years before they were restored. In 1920, as teachers were struggling with rampant postwar inflation, the CTF sought a salary increase to help members deal with their economic woes.[8]

Although there was a consensus in the CTF on the organization's economic program, Haley and Goggin felt that certain structural changes were needed in order for the leaders to be able effectively to pursue their goals. As I have already suggested, members were not so certain that these changes were needed. Thus, almost from the beginning, a gap existed between leaders and led in the CTF that was also present in other labor organizations as they attempted to fulfill organizational goals in the context of a modernizing society. Effective organizational activity required strong leaders who could control activities and persuade the membership to accept their plans and programs. Opposition from the membership, while healthy from a democratic or representative point of view, was looked upon by most leaders as detrimental to the success of the organization. Warren Van Tine has described these early leaders as labor bureaucrats, who shaped their unions to pursue organizational efficiency at the expense of the concerns of dissident members.[9]

A close look at the early history of the CTF shows that Haley and Goggin followed such a pattern. Shortly after the CTF was formed, they began a year-long struggle to control it. Their general program called for a more aggressive set of policies for the federation, but many members supported the current more passive social orientation. Haley and Goggin used rather questionable parliamentary tactics that culminated in their own election to high executive office, and, building on this victory, they pushed through a new method of conducting CTF business which emphasized committees and committee reports in place of the old method of conducting business on the floor of meetings of the membership at large. This interposition of a committee structure between members and final decisions increased the power of federation officers. In particular it increased the president's power by giving her the authority to appoint committee members, and thus decreased the membership's role in initiating policies.[10]

In 1900, another crucial step in organizational development was taken. Haley and Goggin, who were then vice-president and president respectively, had begun to devote a great deal of their time to the pursuit of teacher welfare. In order to enable them to devote all of their time to federation activities, Haley and Goggin were released from teaching and paid salaries with CTF funds equal to those they earned as teachers. Neither ever returned to the classroom. They had embarked on careers as union leaders, and their designation as business agent (Haley) and financial secretary (Goggin) a few years later marked still another stage in organizational development. No longer was the CTF run by elected officers. It was now effectively under the control of two professional leaders occupying staff positions. Haley and Goggin next moved quickly to cut off any opposition. In addition to creating committees, they centralized the election of federation officers, changing the place of election of vice-presidents from district meetings to the general membership meeting. They thus eliminated the districts as breeding grounds for independent leaders who might challenge their own policies. They also increased their personal power by obtaining the right to speak for the teachers before outside groups and to give information to the press in the name of

72

the federation. The financial costs of increased power and status for the CTF leaders were borne by the members, and they were not inconsiderable. Shortly after the creation of staff offices for Haley and Goggin, membership dues increased 100 percent.[11]

All of these activities suggest that Haley and Goggin, though bitter opponents of centralization in school, state, and national politics, and in NEA affairs (as we will see in chapter 5), understood the necessity of centralization in the CTF for the effective pursuit of the organization's objectives. Robert Reid has suggested that this reveals an inconsistency or anomaly in the relationship between Haley's ideology and her actual practices, but if one recognizes that material benefit was the major goal of the CTF and its leaders, the anomaly disappears. When centralization served teachers' economic and organizational interests, it was enhanced; when centralization put those interests in danger, it was opposed. With a centralized structure, Haley and Goggin were free to look after the interests of the teachers as a whole, a special necessity in big-city school systems. The federation could maintain an office that was open every day. The CTF "was accepted as an essential part of the business of the city, just as the Board of Trade, the City Hall, or even the Board of Education itself."[12]

The publication of a federation magazine was an especially important step in creating an effective CTF. The CTF *Bulletin* resembled a trade-union publication more than it did other teacher-oriented periodicals. While typical teachers' journals were filled with discussions of exam questions, teaching aids, literary items, and the like, the *Bulletin* was devoted to salaries, pensions, and federation political battles. Its intent was to educate—or propagandize—the membership regarding the value of the organization's goals and the methods chosen to pursue them. It repeatedly brought the names and activities of Haley and Goggin before its readers and reported the benefits these leaders and their policies had secured.[13]

73

According to Van Tine, one consequence of the bureaucratization of labor organizations was a certain estrangement between union leaders and union members, and it is true that this estrangement surfaced at several points in the CTF's early history. Haley's own autobiography gives further evidence of a gulf between leader and led. She expressed frustration at the frequent opposition to her work by her own membership, teachers "so hampered by the traditions of the past of kowtowing to men and to wealth and position that they haven't attained the status of thinking women." She added that many of Chicago's female teachers were oblivious to the issues involved in CTF fights: they never really knew what was going on. "They live[d] in a corner and they went their way and were about as ignorant of what was going on as beetles under the ground." For Haley and other CTF leaders, members were sometimes a necessary evil, people who stood to benefit from organizational actions but would be better off if they stayed out of the leaders' way and did what they were asked. Responding to a complaint from a Milwaukee leader that members did not attend meetings and participate in association affairs, another CTF leader noted that this was typical of all organizations and indicated nothing about their effectiveness. Effectiveness came with a committed and intelligent leadership.[14]

The pursuit of teacher welfare thrust the CTF into unprecedented situations that earned the group national notoriety. Margaret Haley quickly gained a reputation as a leader who would use extraordinary methods to pursue federation goals. She first exhibited her inclination for controversial action when, in response to a salary cut, she and Catherine Goggin undertook an investigation of tax abuses in the city of Chicago in the late 1890s. The two teachers carefully examined municipal records and uncovered numerous cases of nonpayment or underassessment in both property and franchise taxes. The main beneficiaries were large corporations, public utilities, and influential large landowners such as the *Chicago Tribune*. Haley doggedly pursued the tax case through court actions and finally achieved a favorable settlement in 1904.[15] Moreover, this widely publicized crusade made her famous in political reform circles. Tom Johnson, the noted progressive mayor of Cleveland, wrote to Haley and Goggin that in exposing tax abuse they were performing a service for the entire nation. Johnson and Haley shared the belief that through tax reform and provisions for direct democracy, the economic and political life of the nation would be freed from the grip of corporate predators. In addition to her courageous use of tax reform, Haley attempted to involve the CTF in the fight for such other reform measures as the initiative, referendum, and equal suffrage.[16]

Unlike Johnson and other political reformers, however, Haley pursued the reform cause with more than political goals in mind. She had to show her membership how democratic political reforms would benefit them in their material struggles. The victory in the tax suit was an excellent case in point for Haley, especially when the extra revenue was used for teachers' salaries. Because the tax case lasted for over five years, it also gave Haley and Goggin numerous opportunities to link the teachers' cause to various progressive political reforms. In 1902, when the city council raised police and firemen's salaries but ignored teachers, Haley told her members that women would get their raise when they got the vote, because they could then exert the same leverage on the council as male city employees. Later that same year, when Haley was unsuccessful in getting the city council to withhold the franchise extension of street railway companies, she turned to the reform solution of municipal ownership, remarking that "municipal ownership was a much better club to hold over the railways to force them to pay their taxes than the withholding of franchise extensions." She also noted in her autobiography that it was easy to get teachers' support when she explained that specific reforms were "a very essential part of our tax fight."[17]

Haley linked municipal ownership of street railways to a similar measure which would directly benefit teachers: popular election of school board members. The battle between the CTF and board members oriented to antiteacher administrative reform gave teachers reason to believe that an elected board would be more sympathetic to their interests, and the fact that women could vote on school issues in Illinois made popular election of board members even more attractive to the largely female CTF. When she ultimately was unsuccessful in her campaign for direct election, Haley turned toward the pragmatic alternative of electing a mayor who would then appoint friendly board members. The CTF therefore vigorously supported Judge Edward F. Dunne's successful mayoral campaign in 1905. Dunne was a noted reformer and a proven friend of the CTF; he was the judge who had ruled in favor of the teachers in the tax suit. In this way, Haley and the CTF thrust themselves firmly into the city political arena. They would maintain that political involvement throughout the coming years. They influenced the appointment of federation friend Ella Flagg Young as school superintendent in 1910, and continued thereafter to support candidates for the board and the city and state school superintendencies.[18]

Haley's first allegiance, however, had to be to federation interests, not to political reform. Opponents of reform understood this fact and tried to use it to blunt her efforts. On one occasion, for example, Haley's advocacy of initiative and referendum in the state legislature was short-circuited by opponents who launched an attack on the Chicago teachers' pension fund, knowing that Haley would be forced to drop political reform in order to protect her teachers' economic interests.[19]

Haley's allegiance to federation concerns sometimes caused friction between her and other political reformers dependent on different constituencies. When the reformer Jane Addams was appointed to the school board, the CTF's initial joyful response soon turned sour. Addams did not agree with the federation's stand against merit pay, preferring a modified merit system. Haley criticized Addams both for deserting teachers on the merit issue and also for failing totally to support them on the pension issue. Similarly, Addams was not happy with Haley's primary allegiance to the federation, especially when it superseded their common commitment to reform. When the teachers won the tax suit, Addams wished to see the additional salary money distributed to all elementary teachers, while Haley felt it belonged only to members of the CTF, the organization which had waged the legal battle. Responding to these and other disputes, Haley came to doubt the commitment to teachers' interests of the nonteacher reformers on the school board. According to Reid, Haley subsequently sought the appointment of board members who, rather than share a reform commitment with the CTF, "would identify more closely with federation policy."[20] Obviously Haley needed first to serve her teacher constituency, while Addams could appeal to the abstract conceptions of fairness in merit, pensions, and pay. Margaret Haley could not afford the luxury of such appeals, even if she had wanted to make them. She needed reform that brought with it tangible gains for teachers. One student of the federation seems to ignore this distinction when he argues that the federation played an active part in liberal movements, going "far beyond an immediate concern over economic issues relating only to their jobs."[21]

The intimate connection between teachers' economic interests and Margaret Haley's reform activities is very evident in the federation's position on the women's suffrage issue, but this issue uncovered once again the gap between Haley's political ideas and those of the CTF membership. Haley was deeply committed personally to the cause of women's suffrage. She was known nationally as a powerful advocate of suffrage; she was widely sought as a speaker; suffragists all over the country frequently wrote her, asking her advice and cooperation in winning teachers over to the cause. The key to converting many women, including teachers, was to show how they would benefit materially from the vote, and Haley was adept at telling teachers nationwide that suffrage was the only way to guarantee equal pay with men and at using the Chicago tax case to demonstrate that women needed the vote to protect their economic position.[22]

Among her own members, Haley used a variety of prosuffrage arguments, most of which pointed to economic gains that would follow attainment of the vote. Most immediately, suffrage would help women in their salary fights with recalcitrant boards by making the boards politically accountable to female teachers. Suffrage also was the only way to guarantee adequate funds for schools, equal pay for female teachers, and a fair number of administrative positions for women. Occasionally Haley also sought to educate the teachers by offering a combination of economic and more feminist or ideologically oriented arguments. She once published a letter from Susan B. Anthony in the *Bulletin* which advocated suffrage on the grounds that it would lead to equal pay. Anthony concluded that even if equal pay were not achieved, suffrage was desirable to ensure both woman's self-respect and man's respect for her.[23]

Yet neither her frequent pragmatic nor occasionally ideological appeals were successful in converting Chicago's teachers to the cause. Evidently she needed to appeal to more traditional political and social beliefs to reach most of her constituency. The CTF leadership therefore sounded a variety of conventional, moralistic themes which linked suffrage to more accepted views of women. Teachers were told, for example, that suffrage would not alter the essentials of a woman's role and character. Suffrage leaders were depicted as fulfilled matrons—"sweet, gracious, noble women"—not frustrated spinsters in search of an outlet. Enacting suffrage would bring considerable moral improvement to political and social life, more humanitarian legislation, and more honest candidates for office. Chicago politics, corrupted by "the absence of the most moral, law abiding, and most nearly unpurchasable of her citizens" from civic affairs, would be cleansed if candidates had to appeal to women "providentially provided with the x ray of intuitional perception." Chicago teachers also heard appeals with nativist and class overtones. They were told that while women from the better classes could not vote, all kinds of questionable men had the franchise. Refined, intelligent, moral women were thus rendered inferior to the basest men. Nonvoters encompassed women, imbeciles, aliens, morons, and criminals. While naturalized immigrants, Negroes, tramps, and illiterates voted, the women who financed almshouses, fed the tramps, and educated the illiterates were disenfranchised.[24]

That teachers were constantly bombarded with appeals, many of which stressed material improvement, conservative morals, or racist attitudes, indicates that Haley was dealing with a membership which was not inclined to agree with her own prosuffrage views. This divergence in commitment meant that Haley often had to sacrifice her own suffrage commitment to CTF concerns. For example, in 1914 she responded to a request for help in a New Jersey suffrage campaign by writing, "I can see no prospect for getting away any time in the near future, much as I would love to be with you and help you in your suffrage work." During that same year, when her support was sought by both factions of the national suffrage movement in the midst of a battle over the political posture that the women should adopt, she made no response to either camp, probably because she was caught up in local battles. At times Haley was so busy with federation matters that she did not even answer her own letters. On most occasions, she seemed relatively content with putting federation business before the cause of suffrage. On one occasion she even advised a Cincinnati teacher to drop suffrage work because it was unpopular and turn, instead, to other methods of achieving teachers' goals.[25] On at least one occasion, however, Haley chose suffrage reform over her organizational activity. Throughout much of 1910 and 1911 she was away from Chicago working in suffrage campaigns, first in California and then in Seattle, Washington. Haley seemed happy to be free from the press of federation business; she wrote often in later years of the joys she experienced during the reform crusades.

The reform climate in California and Seattle spurred Haley to write vividly in her autobiography of her own Chicago tax campaign. She hoped to publish her story, believing that publication would have two beneficial results. In the first place, the tax reform story would educate teachers to the merit of vigorously pursuing their own cause, and particularly Chicago's teachers, "who never fully appreciated the value of their crusade." Second, publication, along with lecture fees which might follow from the book's success, would make Haley and the CTF office financially independent. No longer would she be subject to the pettiness and penuriousness of a membership which was neither knowledgeable about nor appreciative of its leaders' efforts.[26] The autobiography, however, was never published and Haley did not get the chance to pursue her work with the financial freedom she desired. Instead, she was forced to continue to justify her actions and programs in ways that made them acceptable to members with values and attitudes considerably different from her own.

The split between Haley and the women who made up the bulk of the CTF membership on the issue of women's suffrage was not confined to Chicago or even to suffrage itself. Female teachers in other organizations around the country were suspicious of their leaders, and often simply because they were women. Carter Alexander reported in 1910 that female teachers generally distrusted female leaders. He attributed this distrust largely to "traditional" views, "arising in general social conditions." He traced the phenomenon back at least to the 1880s and noted that until the distrust was removed, few women would be successful as leaders of teachers' associations.[27]

Affiliation with organized labor was an even more volatile issue separating Haley from a substantial portion of the CTF membership than was women's suffrage. Haley took the CTF into the Chicago Federation of Labor in 1902, but not without serious objections from many members. Salary difficulties early in the 1902–3 school year precipitated the CTF's affiliation with labor, as they did many other of the group's actions. In any case, Haley felt that the teachers had much to gain politically from joining with labor. She wrote in her autobiography that

> the teachers were a body of non voters trying to cope with the political situation with no political power and . . . affiliation with a large group of voters, whose children were in the public schools and whose interests in the schools were through the children, was a very much needed element of strength to the teachers in their struggle.

Labor had already aided the teachers in the tax reform campaign, and one labor leader invited the teachers to follow up this earlier cooperation by formal affiliation, thereby giving "to the 200,000 affiliated workingmen and voters of Chicago, the right to take up the cause of the teachers and the children."[28]

At the time the teachers considered an official relationship with labor, however, the workers themselves seemed in no position to respond unanimously to any political issue. Chicago labor, then as well as later, was powerful in numbers but split over the issue of political action. Union leaders feared political involvement because it might develop conflicts among various groups of union members, and a battle between a corrupt building trades faction and a reform group for control of the labor movement added to the difficulties. However, personal and ideological ties between Margaret Haley and John Fitzpatrick, leader of the reform faction in labor, cemented the union between labor and the teachers at the top organizational levels. Fitzpatrick was a committed political reformer who supported most of the measures for which Haley worked. The close personal relationship which developed between Haley and Fitzpatrick probably was facilitated by Fitzpatrick's wife, who happened to be not only an elementary-school teacher but also a member of the CTF.[29]

Despite collaboration between the labor and teacher leaders, the CTF membership did not share Haley's enthusiasm for the workers. When the federation considered affiliation, Haley's and Goggin's arguments in favor of it were answered by the elected president of the CTF, who stated that her opposition was not to the labor movement, but to teachers' affiliating with only one class of the population. The public schools were to serve all classes, not just the organized workers. Opponents also voiced their fear that affiliation would mean a strike. Fitzpatrick himself answered this objection in a letter to the teachers which assured them that the Chicago Federation of Labor had no power to call a strike and could not dictate the policy of any affiliated organization. Nevertheless, the opposition did not yield easily. At a meeting called to discuss the merits and demerits of affiliation, Jane Addams spoke in favor of unionization and tipped the balance of member opinion in favor of it. Haley seized the opportunity and immediately pushed affiliation through, though not without some cost. The CTF lost its president and an undetermined but large number of its total membership through resignations.[30]

Despite these losses, affiliation almost immediately paid tangible dividends. Within a month of their vote to join labor, elementary-school teachers received a fifty-dollar raise. Haley herself understood that economic benefits were the most important reasons for teachers to join labor. She told Buffalo teachers who were considering joining labor that both teachers and laborers benefited practically from affiliation. Teachers gained labor's political clout and workers gained an intelligent voice which would help them determine how to use their political power effectively. This, she said, was how things worked in Chicago.[31]

Despite Haley's enthusiastic and persistent attempts to educate CTF members in the benefits of allying with labor, opposition did not disappear. The CTF turned down a 1906 appeal from typographical workers to publicize their strike among teachers with the explanation, "While we are in sympathy with you the fight in our own organization has been so fierce that it does not seem prudent to invite further attacks such as the insertion of this item would do." Haley sometimes indicated the delicacy of her own situation to her labor allies. She told Fitzpatrick that the labor people should not "fail to understand the difficulty of the teachers joining hands with the labor unions." She added that the big-business opponents of teachers and workers understood teacher reluctance to affiliate quite well, and that labor, if it wished to aid teacher leaders who supported affiliation, had best be sensitive to the difficulties those leaders encountered in getting across the labor message.[32] Evidently a reservoir of antilabor sentiment remained in the CTF, even some years after affiliation.

By 1915, the antilabor faction had developed considerable influence within the Chicago board of education. Jacob Loeb, the acknowledged leader of the antilabor board members, took it upon himself to rid the Chicago schools of the labor menace in the teaching force. The CTF and the Loeb members of the school board clashed initially over a reported deficit of six hundred thousand dollars in the school budget; Loeb used it to launch an investigation of economy and efficiency in the schools. The investigation yielded a number of solutions for the financial crisis, the most notable of which was a salary cut for teachers. The CTF responded by working with Superintendent Ella Flagg Young to come up with an alternative to salary cuts, and they were successful in obtaining a tax increase from the state legislature. The board nevertheless proceeded with its original plans and failed to implement them only because the CTF organized vocal political opposition.[33]

Temporarily stymied, the board regrouped for another assault on organized teachers. In August 1915, a board committee chaired by Loeb recommended that no teacher be employed who belonged to an organization which affiliated with labor or which employed full-time paid staff who were not teaching in the schools. The specific target of the committee was Haley and the CTF, but the broad wording of Loeb's recommendation inadvertently banned several other groups, including any which were affiliated with the state teachers' association. An amended second version spoke specifically to the CTF and its affiliation with organized labor, but the CTF and other labor-affiliated teachers' groups (male and female high-school teachers' federations) managed to blunt both Loeb rules by obtaining court injunctions against their enforcement.[34]

The Loeb forces again regrouped and began a new attack in June 1916. As the time neared for the annual rehiring of every teacher, the board sent shock waves through the teaching force by successfully obtaining a judicial reversal of the tenure provision which had accompanied the enactment of pension legislation in the 1890s. Acting on this warrant, the board voted not to rehire sixty-eight teachers for the 1916–17 school year, thirty-eight of whom were CTF officers and members. Clearly the board intended to break the CTF. All of the CTF members had been rated good or above by their superiors, while several of the thirty other teachers not rehired had received unsatisfactory ratings. Jacob Loeb's election to the board chairmanship further indicated that the board was now at war with the CTF.[35]

Haley and her group, supported vigorously by the local federation of labor, continued to battle the board in the press and in local and state legislative bodies. This time, however, the board held the upper hand. The 1916–17 school year began without the dismissed teachers, and teachers received further bad news from an October 1916 court decision reversing the earlier injunctions and upholding the Loeb rules against labor affiliation and paid staff for teachers' organizations. The CTF responded by pushing new tenure legislation through the city council and state legislature. In April 1917, the legislature enacted a tenure provision for Chicago's teachers which was, at best, a mixed blessing. Though tenure was granted, the CTF had to accept several other provisions contrary to its long-held desires. The superintendent won a four-year term of office, thereby greatly increasing his own power, and the school board, though smaller, was still to be appointed by the mayor, not elected by the voters. Teachers could not even be sure of the tenure provision granted by the legislature, since one day before the bill's final passage a court decision upheld the dismissal of the sixty-eight teachers with language that cast doubt on the new tenure law.[36]

While all this legal and legislative maneuvering was going on, the CTF took action to prepare for either victory or defeat by the Loeb board. Ignoring the Loeb rules, Haley's group joined the Illinois State Federation of Labor in the fall of 1915 and helped form the AFT in early 1916. Three of the four founding AFT locals were made up of Chicago teachers, the CTF and the male and female high-school teachers' organizations. On the other hand, the CTF leaders were also planning for the possibility of a Loeb victory. A new constitution proposed for the group in 1916 substituted the word "organization" for "federation" wherever it appeared in the old document. Later in the year, a letter from Haley to a local labor leader about the Loeb rules contained the following handwritten postscript: "Jacob Loeb has stated within 3 weeks (to Alderman Thos. Lynch) but you must not use his name—that the teachers can get back by withdrawing from the Federation of Labor."[37]

Court sanction of both the Loeb rule on labor affiliation and the firing of the sixty-eight teachers meant that the CTF was in a precarious position. Actions by individual members and the membership as a whole intensified the crisis. Ida Fursman, president of the federation and one of the dismissed teachers, expressed her own doubts about the organization's position.

> I do think the time to compromise on the best terms we can possibly make has come. . . . We cannot afford to be obstinate or obdurate but must meet those in authority on a common ground. I feel that the detachment [the 68 teachers] has stood all they possibly can from the strain of the past year.

Another of "the detachment" also urged compromise with the board. "When the olive branch is offered to us, even if it is not the best, we should take it and the world will stand back of us." She went on to argue that the CTF had little choice because "the teachers as a whole are not standing back of us," and if the compromise were not accepted, "the rank and file of the teachers will withdraw their membership and financial aid." This was no idle comment; federation membership in 1917 had dropped considerably from its pre-Loeb figure of five thousand.[38]

Faced with a legal defeat and a demoralized membership, many of whom were never staunch labor supporters in the first place, Haley and the CTF leadership prepared to withdraw from the labor movement in order to gain reinstatement of the fired teachers and preservation of the federation as an unaffiliated organization. Fitzpatrick and the labor federation also faced the inevitable by approving the CTF withdrawal. On 21 May 1917, the CTF announced it was leaving the Chicago Federation of Labor, the Illinois State Federation of Labor, the AFT, and the Women's Trade Union League. On 13 June, the board rehired the dismissed teachers, indicating that its war with the CTF was over. The official labor career of the CTF had ended, as it had begun, because of practical priorities.[39]

Students of the federation have offered several explanations for its withdrawal from the labor movement, many of which stress reasons not apparent in the official accounts. Robert Reid and Mary Herrick both allude to ethnicity and religion, Reid suggesting that Haley, an Irish Catholic and an anglophobe, left labor because it was led by the Englishman Samuel Gompers and because of its pro-British policies before the beginning of World War I. The anonymous author of the "Inventory of the Chicago Teachers' Federation Papers" stressed a wavering of the ideological commitment of teachers to labor or labor to teachers, arguing that either teachers first abandoned the reform commitment they shared with labor and then withdrew, or that labor did not wholeheartedly support the fired teachers, thereby hastening the withdrawal.[40] None of these explanations can be conclusively documented. The simpler, documented rationale is the one presented here, which stresses the practical and pragmatic forces at work in both the affiliation and the withdrawal.

Margaret Haley's prime goals were to achieve practical benefits and maintain the CTF as an organization. When organizational welfare conflicted with her own commitment to suffrage reform, she deemphasized that commitment. Similarly, when the necessity of maintaining her organization and her own leadership was at stake, she was willing to withdraw from labor. In 1926, she explained that she compromised on the ideological issue of labor affiliation in order to save the CTF. The Loeb rule forbade both labor affiliation and full-time leaders who were not school employees; circumventing the latter prohibition was far more important to Haley.

> The other provision of the Loeb rule which forbade affiliation with labor was promulgated for public consumption, but the teeth and claws of the Loeb rule were in the provision that forbade teachers to maintain an organization that had officers not under the control of the Board of Education.

Withdrawing from labor allowed the CTF to survive with its leadership and its organizational structure intact. Haley went on to say that John Fitzpatrick understood these realities and recommended withdrawal as the best practical alternative available. Neither he nor Haley expected that withdrawal would mean the end of cooperation between the elementary teachers and organized labor. And, of course, it did not.[41] The two leaders and their organizations continued to work together, unofficially but almost as closely as before.

Differences between Margaret Haley, the labor militant and reformer, and the leadership of the APSTA described in chapter 2 appear less stark once one has recognized the primacy of pragmatic and organizational issues. The Atlanta organization pursued goals similar to those of its Chicago counterpart, although not as vigorously. This difference, however, seems more explainable in terms of the social contexts in which the groups acted than by reference to inherent differences between the groups themselves. The cautious APSTA existed in a town far more conservative, both politically and socially, than Chicago. The organizational structure of the two groups, though different in many respects, was similar in intent and effect. Though Atlanta had no single leader like Haley, it circulated leadership of the teachers' association among a small group of administrators and experienced teachers who carefully controlled the organization and guarded against unpredictable membership-initiated activities. For both groups and both sets of leaders, the essential goal was economic—job-related benefits for the members— and the essential means of reaching that goal was an organizational structure suited to pursuing those benefits in the local political and social environment.

Leaders from many teacher organizations throughout the country were frustrated, like Margaret Haley, by the hesitancy with which members embraced the cause. Reports from various campaigns for teacher benefits noted that "the hardest work is overcoming the apathy or active opposition of other teachers." The state teachers' association in New Jersey, after the successful culmination of a seventeen-year-long fight for pensions, could testify that its hardest tasks were "arousing apathetic teachers" and "placating those actively opposed" to the cause.[42] Let us now look at the organized teachers in New York and see how the situation in the nation's largest city resembled or differed from circumstances elsewhere.

4

Teachers' Organizations in
New York City, 1905–1920

New York was by far the largest and most cosmopolitan of American cities in the early twentieth century. This size and diversity had several effects on the city's teachers' organizations. Sheer size, particularly after the consolidation of the schools in the boroughs into one system in the late 1890s, meant that there were enough teachers to support separate organizations for teachers in the primary grades, in the grammar grades, for elementary-school principals, for high-school teachers of different subjects, and for high-school principals.[1] The extreme specialization which characterized teachers' associations in New York was present to a lesser degree in other large cities like Chicago, but absent in most smaller cities like Atlanta. Nevertheless, teachers did not give up the borough orientation which had characterized teachers' associations and most aspects of the city's life in the nineteenth century. As late as the 1930s, the borough associations were still healthy, enrolling between 40 and 50 percent of the eligible staff (who often also belonged to a subject-matter or grade-level association).[2] A lack of documentary evidence makes detailed study of these borough associations impossible, but their longevity alone indicates that twentieth-century New York

89

teachers strongly preferred, as had their colleagues in the 1890s, the ties of a local-oriented past to whatever benefits citywide groups of teachers chose to pursue.

In spite of this demonstrated preference of teachers for borough associations alongside of specialized subject-matter and grade-level associations, the best-known early-twentieth-century New York City teachers' organizations are the Teachers' League and its successor, the Teachers' Union. The league's notoriety arises from its lively participation in the political debates of its time. Scholars of such diverse ideological backgrounds as the Marxist Celia Zitron and the liberal Philip Taft have copiously documented and argued about the league's socialist politics and educational reform ideas.[3] The plethora of information available about the league, combined with the lack of information available on other teachers' groups, has resulted in a false image of the radical Teachers' League as representative of early-twentieth-century teachers' organizations.

The Teachers' League could have prospered as a citywide teachers' organization only in a setting as cosmopolitan as New York, with its multiplicity of ethnic groups and its wide range of intellectual and political ideas. The league's relative lack of success in enrolling eligible members is the main reason for believing that it did not represent the beliefs or goals of most New York City teachers. Exact membership counts do not exist, but informed estimates put the total number at between eight hundred and fifteen hundred through the organization's first two decades. In 1932, twenty years after the league was founded, New York had 36,000 teachers, making the most generous estimate of its membership less than 5 percent of those eligible. These are not impressive figures.[4]

The reasons for the league's relatively low membership are many and varied. Ethnicity was certainly a factor. Names on the early membership rolls indicate that the group was heavily Jewish, surely an impediment to membership among largely Anglo-Saxon and Irish Catholic elementary-school

90

teachers. League members also were mostly male and mostly high-school teachers, another certain obstacle to allegiance by the predominantly female elementary-school teaching force. Finally, the socialist politics and radical educational ideas of the league leadership alienated most of New York's teachers, just as they would have alienated teachers in Chicago or Atlanta.[5]

One citywide teachers' organization had much greater success in enrolling a significant number of teachers. That group, the Interborough Association of Women Teachers (IAWT) counted fourteen thousand members in 1910.[6] The IAWT, by devoting itself to the single goal of equal pay for female teachers, proved far more successful than the Teachers' League in overcoming the twin obstacles of borough orientation and orientation to place in the city's complicated occupational hierarchy. The fact that women greatly outnumbered men among New York's teachers should not be ignored, yet the league should not have ruled the fight of the female teachers for equal pay out of its own program, for that fight was intimately related to the political reform of women's suffrage. Female teachers, however, seldom showed interest in political reforms.

Unlike the teachers' organizations in Atlanta and Chicago, which were founded to pursue a range of economic goals, the IAWT was a single-purpose organization. It was founded in April 1906 with the specific goal of attaining salaries for female teachers that would be equal to those of their male colleagues. Its initial efforts were concentrated in the city's board of education. Unsuccessful with board members, the IAWT then took its fight to the state legislature, the body ultimately responsible for funding the city schools. In 1907, the legislature approved a bill for equal pay, but it was vetoed by George B. McClellan, the mayor of New York City—who also was the brother-in-law of the school board president who had vigorously opposed equal pay. The legislature overrode his veto, but the bill was then vetoed by Governor Hughes. In 1908, the equal-pay measure passed one house of the legislature but was held in committee in the other house by the Republican majority. In 1909, the 1907 experience of legislative passage and mayoral veto was repeated. In 1910, however, the IAWT began a successful push, aided by a fluid political situation involving city charter reform and by the election of a mayor favorable to its cause. In 1911, the equal-pay law was finally approved by city officials, the state legislature, and the governor.[7]

Although it was successful in obtaining the necessary legislation for equal pay, the IAWT was not totally to achieve its goal for several more years. The 1911 law was violated in practice often enough to necessitate passage of another equal-pay law in 1923, and this law too was not well enforced. Yet the IAWT's achievement should not be overlooked. It represented a significant symbolic victory for female teachers in New York, and the importance of this victory was grasped by both women and men nationwide.[8]

A closer look at the structure of the IAWT, the ideology of its leadership, the tactics it used to achieve passage of the equal-pay law, and the personal goals of its leaders will demonstrate that the IAWT practiced a conservative feminism as it pursued its occupational goals. This conservatism made the organization palatable to New York's female teachers, who shared much of the traditionalism of their Atlanta and Chicago counterparts.

The IAWT, like the Teachers' League and any other New York teachers' organization claiming to represent a citywide constituency, had to contend with its members' tendency to think of themselves as teachers in one of the city's boroughs, not in the city itself. This borough identification was an organizational problem from the beginning, when in 1906 the membership split on whether the president should be from Brooklyn or Manhattan. The dispute was settled in favor of the Manhattan candidate, primarily because she was a classroom teacher, not an administrator. Shortly after the election, however, it was discovered that she was not in fact a classroom teacher, but rather a department head who was paid by the board at a principal's rate. Yet the election results were not reversed, indicating either that teacher-administrator conflict was not a serious issue or that executive office carried with it the power to head off attempts at recall.[9]

The IAWT's first organizational structure attempted to mitigate borough divisiveness by establishing a vice-president for each borough and locating some activities in the boroughs. With the election of Grace Strachan to the presidency in 1907, however, the IAWT embarked on its legislative campaign for equal pay, an issue that effectively overshadowed borough identification. The IAWT's frequent lobbying in the legislature gave the organization a public prominence seldom achieved by any of its predecessors or competitors. The publicity garnered by the lobbyists, particularly Grace Strachan, caused great discomfort to the city's educational and political leaders. Their clumsy attempts at reprimanding Strachan and other IAWT lobbyists served to strengthen the teachers' conviction that the IAWT was on the right track.[10]

Born in Buffalo and educated at that city's normal school, Strachan taught in Buffalo's elementary and high schools before coming to New York. She quickly moved up in the New York educational hierarchy, serving one year as a teacher, moving to a faculty position at the teachers' training school, then to a principalship and an associate superintendency, and finally to a district superintendency. This rapid rise testifies both to Strachan's abilities and to her facility at mastering the internal politics of the city schools. It also indicates the degree to which an astute, ambitious teacher could overcome the seniority system that teachers had fought so hard to protect in the 1890s. Moreover, Strachan's political skills and interests were not confined to the arena of the school system, as her vigorous lobbying illustrated. In September 1907, the board of education, upset at the teachers' refusal to accept the board's no answer on equal pay as final and astounded at their audacity in taking the issue to the legislature, censured several IAWT members who took days off from school to lobby in Albany. Grace Strachan, absent for a total of thirty-four days during the 1906–7 school year, was the board's main target. Censure by the board carried no penalty, the members having voted against stronger disciplinary measures, but it did serve to put teachers on notice that the board disapproved of their activity and would frown upon a repetition of it.[11]

If the board expected Strachan and the IAWT to heed its warnings, it was in for a disappointment. One month after the censure, Strachan was elected president of the IAWT, and she vowed publicly to continue lobbying for equal pay. Strachan and her membership followed up on their promise in 1908, when they escalated their political tactics by urging teachers to support the opponent of the governor who had vetoed the 1907 equal-pay bill. This prompted another board investigation of "electioneering" by the teachers and a proposed board amendment to the school statutes which prohibited political activity by teachers. This amendment was ultimately defeated, but not before the doings of Strachan and her teachers were thoroughly aired in both the board meetings and the city newspapers. A prominent local minister charged that Strachan and the IAWT, by supporting a gubernatorial candidate who did not oppose gambling, had entered into an unholy conspiracy with gamblers and their allies, the city's Tammany machine politicians. Strachan responded, not by denying the charge of an unholy alliance, but by defending the teachers' actions on pragmatic grounds. They had cooperated with a candidate who supported their fight for equal pay. His other positions were of less concern to them, and their support of him certainly did not imply support of all his policies.[12]

Strachan was a careful and consummate political maneuverer who astutely managed her organization's fight to achieve its single objective. If this struggle involved espousing one political position at one time and a contradictory position at another time, she would do it. In 1907, for instance, Strachan could argue for a bill which advocated equal pay along with locating salary responsibility in the city school board by noting that the bill supported the principle of home rule. A few years later she would argue, in a direct contradiction of the principle of home rule, that a mayor's veto of an equal-pay bill was dubious because education was a state function.[13] Sometimes her single-mindedness caused her to view even educational issues according to whether or not they supported the equal-pay principle. For instance, she favored a six-year elementary school and six-year high school proposal not on its educational merits, but

> in so far as it establishes the principle that the positions in the school department should be carefully graded, that one salary should be attached to each grade of position, and then that the person occupying any of these positions should receive the salary attached to the position, regardless of sex.[14]

Her unwavering devotion to equal pay and the political machinations and compromises she undertook to achieve it encouraged Strachan's enemies to depict her as a kind of one-woman educational Tammany Hall. On several occasions her own actions abetted that image. For example, in 1907 Strachan and some of her IAWT members broke up and took over a meeting of another teachers' association made up of female primary-grade teachers who felt that equal pay would do them little good, since few if any men taught in the lower grades. According to one account, Strachan "entered the room and advanced to the platform followed by about 500 supporters." The IAWT women then demanded that Strachan be allowed to speak and disrupted the other organization's effort to continue with its agenda. At one point, "Mrs. Lenihan and Miss Strachan shoved their way through the crowd to the platform, demanding to be heard. Disorder followed. Miss Strachan stood near the chairman's desk, tapping her pencil and looking angry." Finally, when it became apparent that the IAWT group would not allow the meeting to go on, the other association moved to another location. The IAWT followed and disrupted that meeting also.[15]

95

Shortly after the equal-pay victory of 1911, a plan to reward Strachan with a sum of money from grateful IAWT members furthered her image as an educational boss. Contributions were solicited from each female teacher in the fall of 1912, and plans were made to present a check to Strachan at the April 1913 IAWT meeting. One report noted that the creation of the fund had caused many members to defect. "There are teachers who do not approve of it and who think that the presentation of money is not the right way to reward Miss Strachan. Many have refused to contribute to the fund for these reasons." Strachan herself seldom referred to the fund and claimed to know nothing about it, though the papers and the IAWT members discussed it freely for over a year.[16]

There can be no doubt, however, that Strachan did seek personal advancement through her IAWT activities. In chapter 5, I will show how she used her equal-pay activities as a basis for her pursuit of the presidency of the NEA in 1912 and again in 1915. In 1912, she linked her own NEA presidential ambitions to those of New York's mayor, the signer of the equal-pay bill who was rumored to be a candidate for the nation's presidency. She also sought higher office in the city schools. As early as 1910, she was rumored to be a possible candidate for the city superintendency. In 1913 she announced her own candidacy for a vacancy which would soon occur among the associate city superintendents. Both Strachan's personal advocacy and the IAWT members' vocal support of her candidacy were unprecedented in city school affairs. Strachan obviously expected her IAWT supporters to carry her through to victory with the same approach they had used in the equal-pay movement, although a year later, when a vacancy did occur, she publicly withdrew from consideration because the mayor opposed her candidacy.[17]

Politics were intimately involved in the IAWT's very reason for being, as well as in the careers of its leaders. As an equal pay for women organization, the IAWT defined itself and was defined by others in relation to suffrage groups and other feminist organizations. When *School* magazine re-counted the victory of the equal-pay forces in 1911, it noted the connections between teachers' pay and suffragism.

> This is a record that reflects the strength of woman's movement in the United States toward a larger sphere of action, responsibilities, and rewards. The equal-pay fight for women school teachers is a part of this world-wide movement and is to be viewed as such, not from the angle of school work. . . . Woman's ability to organize, direct and control popular movements among her own sex has not been more strikingly illustrated of recent years than in the public school system of New York City.

The activity of IAWT leaders such as Katherine Blake in both the equal-pay and the city and state suffrage movements testifies further to the intimate tie between the two groups.[18]

Suffragists came from a wide range of political back-grounds, with a principled egalitarian feminism at one end of the spectrum and a conservative nonegalitarianism at the other. Aileen Kraditor has observed that while most nine-teenth-century suffragists had argued for the cause on the basis of equal justice and rights for women, their early twen-tieth-century successors began to sound newer themes which ignored egalitarian principles. As suffrage came to be a real-izable goal instead of simply a moral crusade, its advocates used arguments geared to appeal to more and more women who might be induced to support suffrage reform if they could avoid making any commitment to the issue of equal rights. It is clear that while the IAWT officially supported suffrage, the members did not embrace equal rights. In 1913, Strachan charged that a female teacher who married was breaking her contract and committing an immoral act. Often the organization would meet to hear addresses from male legislators who praised the women for their political activity in words upholding traditional views of male-female relation-ships. For example, the official IAWT book on the equal-pay campaign quoted approvingly one state legislator's description of the women's fight: "The chivalric spirit of man cannot but be inspired by the plucky battle which is being waged."[19]

Another attitude that IAWT members shared with some suffragists was suspicion of immigrants. In the same spirit that caused conservative women suffragists to complain of the unfairness of their being denied the vote while ignorant male immigrants enjoyed it, the IAWT dismissed the anti-feminist views of foreign-born teachers by arguing that the immigrant males did not deserve a hearing "on account of their lack of long and familiar acquaintance with us and our institutions."[20]

At the tactical level, twentieth-century conservative suffragists began to link their campaign to issues and arguments which would stress the materially expedient reasons for women to support the cause. The equal-pay campaign is a prototype of this expediency-oriented suffragism and Grace Strachan's style was characteristic of the conservative female leader. She shared her political realism, strong-arm tactics, penchant for patronage, and thirst for personal advancement with other early twentieth-century leaders of the women's movement. Strachan described herself as "a woman who has simply and honorably, without thought of self-aggrandizement or self-advancement or self-suffering worked for the establishment of a moral principle," but the following description, which contrasts expediency-oriented suffragists with their egalitarian predecessors, more accurately characterizes her and her activities.

> When victories could be won here and there at the cost of small concessions to political expediency, the hard facts of political life and the equivocal position of middle class women in American society pulled them away from the high ideals and ringing declarations [of their predecessors]. To win support from needed allies they compromised perhaps more than the requirements of alliances dictated. More often than not they voiced the ideals and advocated the compromises at the same time.[21]

Strachan's feminism also may be profitably contrasted with Margaret Haley's. While Strachan would use suffrage arguments in conjunction with her fight for equal pay, she gave little evidence of commitment to suffragism or any other political reform outside the context of more pay for teachers. Haley, however, worked for suffrage and other social and political reforms inside and outside of the teachers' movement. Yet Strachan did share with Haley a talent for effective political infighting. Moreover, the IAWT and CTF members had a mutual desire for the tangible economic benefits which emerged from the political fights waged by their leaders. That Haley and Strachan were successful, despite the differences in their political beliefs, testifies both to the variety of leadership styles and to the similarity of goals which permeated local teachers' organizations in this period. We can better understand the variety of early teacher leaders by next examining the New York teachers' union and then contrasting it with the IAWT.

The Teachers' League was founded in February 1913. Henry R. Linville was its first president and a major leader, along with Abraham Lefkowitz, throughout its early years. For one year before the league was formed, Linville edited a paper devoted to the schools, the *American Teacher*. Planning for the league began in January 1913, with small meetings of teachers "representing the various radical interests." The slogan developed in these early meetings, "Democracy in Education," also appeared on the masthead of the *American Teacher*. The major specific democratic change that the organizers advocated was the election of teacher representatives to the board of education.[22]

The Teachers' League held its initial meeting at Teachers College, Columbia University, in late February 1913. John Dewey, the suffragist Charlotte Perkins Gilman, and other local notables appeared as speakers, and they drew some seven hundred teachers to the meeting. When the speeches were over and the time for formal organization of the group

99

was at hand, however, only seventy teachers remained to hear the league announce its purposes: to give teachers a voice and vote in determining school policies, to give them representatives on the board of education, to help settle school problems, to eliminate politics from the school system (particularly from promotions), and to encourage free public discussion of educational issues. Salaries and other economic issues were conspicuously absent from this list. Moreover, controversy flared, first when Grace Strachan objected to the idea of teachers on boards, and again when some teachers objected to Linville's proposal to make his paper the official organ of the Teachers' League. Linville firmly controlled the meeting, however, and he overruled objections from the floor on the issues of his paper, the makeup of the executive committee, and the number of members required for a quorum. One local school paper noted the organization's failure to attract many members, but praised its goals of publicizing and discussing school issues, remarking that discussions would clarify issues in the public mind. But, perhaps knowing Linville's political orientation, the paper also cautioned, "If the leaders are over zealous they may do more harm than good."[23]

At its second meeting, the league sought to distinguish itself from all other teachers' organizations. While groups like the IAWT and organizations of male teachers "focussed their attention chiefly on obtaining increases in salaries for themselves," the league would work for better working conditions for teachers and better education for children. When the Teachers' League changed its name to the Teachers' Union and formally affiliated with the American Federation of Labor (AFL) in March 1916, both Linville and the original educational and political emphasis remained. The new union's aims were similar to those of the league: the protection of teachers' legal interests, the maintenance of their right to protection from oppressive supervision, and the promotion of democratic education in the schools. Linville's own speech at the first union meeting denounced overcrowding in the

100

schools, the employment of substitutes at low pay while regular teachers went unemployed, other irregularities in teacher employment, and the generally hostile attitude to the schools of the New York City Board of Estimate. These specifics indicate that though Linville was by then paying some attention to the teachers' financial situation, he considered it primarily as an injustice in board and city policy.[24]

Attendance at the first union meeting indicated that the new organization was somewhat more attractive to teachers than the league had been. More than a thousand teachers were members, and *School* described them as comprising teachers who were "not in love with principals or superintendents." Militant speeches were made, with one speaker from the Women's Trade Union League arguing that principals should be excluded from the union. *School* attributed the large attendance at the meeting to the teachers' fear that the city government was about to obtain control of the schools. Teachers, whose salaries were then governed by state legislation, faced the prospect of being reduced to city employees subject to the whims of the Board of Estimate and the city controller. This drove them into the arms of labor. According to *School*, however, the union would have trouble increasing its initial membership because of its radical program and rhetoric. Teachers were not likely to abandon the IAWT and the other teachers' associations, which had sought and won tangible benefits, in favor of an unproved organization which led with slogans. While levelheaded leadership could bring about cooperation with other teachers' associations, the militance and antisupervisor rhetoric of the union speakers was not encouraging. Teachers who sought to encourage discipline in schoolchildren were not likely to approve of teachers' unions which stood against organizational discipline in the schools. The union's subsequent lack of success in increasing its membership suggests that this prediction was correct.[25]

The membership shortage the union experienced in its early years was due mainly to the political orientation of Linville and his fellow union activists. As Linville's democratic socialism increasingly permeated the pages of the *American Teacher*, teachers came to associate the union with radical politics. After the United States entered World War I, the controversy in socialist circles over whether or not to support the war effort further tainted the teachers' union as an antiwar group, particularly when it chose to defend three antiwar high-school teachers. By January 1918, the New York union had experienced a 60 percent loss in membership, and its leaders acknowledged that the loss was due to pacifist activity. In September of the same year, Linville could see that the membership situation was worsening. Even in schools which were union strongholds, members were waiting to pay dues until the union indicated what it was going to do for their salaries. Thus, the union added unresponsiveness to economic issues to its antiwar reputation among city teachers.[26]

Linville's personal response to the membership decline indicates that he preferred a union which maintained its militant reforming, labor, socialist stance to one which served the material interests of teachers, even at the expense of losing members. In 1917, in the midst of the war controversies and a rampant inflation which was costing teachers dearly, Linville described the greatest problem in the New York schools as the same one which he stressed five years earlier.

> Our great evil is cruel supervision. We have characterized it as *inhuman*. Promotions to the higher positions are made on the basis of favoritism. . . . I think you should realize that we have been with our problem for many years, and have had not a little experience in organizing ideas and methods of doing things for the purpose of advancing our profession. In a word we have, I think, attained the standing of experts in reform of this kind.

He went on to note that another matter occupying his and the union's time was the "lack of professional standing on the part of many of our high school principals." He had proposed to an associate superintendent that incompetent principals be dismissed and followed up with a plea for the removal of several specific individuals. While Linville summed up the union's platform as a "campaign for educational regeneration," most teachers were concerned not for regeneration, but for economic survival.[27]

Despite all of his ideological priorities, Linville was no fool. Late in 1918, he began to concentrate on the teachers' economic crisis. He asked a national AFT organizer for some labor speakers to address a mass union meeting opening a salary campaign. Yet one month later, an influential member resigned because of the political orientation of the union and its paper. He attacked an article Linville wrote about the Industrial Workers of the World, a group most teachers thought of as revolutionaries; in replying, Linville remarked that just as he had sought justice for teachers, he would demand justice for the IWW. Similarly, he would demand and continue to demand justice for dissident radical teachers like the high-school teachers under fire for their opposition to the war. Responding to a charge that he was too socialistic and politically involved, Linville denied the charge of socialism but defended his union's political involvement. "As teachers we should be more than teachers,—surely you would not disapprove of our strengthening ourselves as citizens and using the added strength for getting the things we want, such as improving our salaries and working conditions." Thus he attempted to show that his controversial ideological commitments were related to material benefits for teachers.[28]

Linville went on to tell this union dissident that labor was working behind the scenes for an increase in teachers' salaries and that a considerable number of the members of another teachers' organization were ready to join the union if the board did not voluntarily grant salary increases. He contrasted the union's campaign for a salary raise with that of another group of teachers who were willing to increase class sizes in order to get a pay increase. "The Union will certainly fight the plan to make the work harder" and would push its own plan as the desirable alternative.[29] In many of these arguments, Linville was being realistic. Teachers' gains in

New York, just as in Atlanta and Chicago, resulted from political activity, but Linville's own politics were not those of most teachers. The union therefore might gain members during brief periods of militancy on economic issues, but the ideological gulf between Linville and the rank-and-file made sustaining those gains difficult.

Besides Linville's penchant for political and educational reform, the union faced other obstacles to building a large membership. Teachers in New York, as elsewhere, were reluctant to affiliate with labor. At the New York union's initial meeting in 1916, trade-union organizers assured hesitant teachers that unions did not mean that teachers would have to strike. Margaret Haley also appeared and told the teachers that labor had helped Chicago's teachers greatly in stopping corporate tax-dodging. Yet teacher hesitancy towards labor affiliation did not diminish. In 1918, Linville told a female labor leader who was to speak before his union that she should be sure to stress the economic reasons for teachers' joining labor. He thought that those who ordinarily would not want to join with workers would be more likely to respond to economic arguments for affiliation. He added that even teachers who already were union members needed better grounding in union principles, and he urged her to tell her listeners how much dues women in other trade unions paid, since many teachers "kick on paying fifty cents a month for the ten school months."[30]

The Teachers' Union, like most teachers' associations, was unable to overcome the balkanization of New York's teachers. Despite its formal posture of representing both sexes and all grade levels, the union could not shake its reputation for being primarily concerned with high-school and male teachers. For example, in 1919, when union stalwart Abraham Lefkowitz was working on a salary bill in the state legislature, Linville wrote to him expressing concern for the salary situation of male elementary-school teachers and continued support for the differential between elementary- and high-school teachers. In 1921, the union concentrated on the salary grievances of the mostly male high-school teachers and also opposed reform of the high schools. Of course, it seems reasonable to conclude that an organization will reflect the problems of its leadership and the majority of its membership. Both Linville and Lefkowitz were high-school teachers. But Linville, who was willing to push so far away from economic interests toward political reform in his general union platform, seemed much less willing to push economically in directions other than those which reflected his own immediate interest as a male high-school teacher. The union never did attract many elementary-school teachers.[31]

Henry Linville, the socialist union leader, was as interested in using his union activities for personal advancement as other less visionary teachers like Grace Strachan. In February 1917, he applied for a high-school principalship in New York, citing his twenty years of school experience and his record as an organizer of both the Teachers' League and the Teachers' Union as an indication of his administrative ability. This pursuit of the principalship seems at the least a partial repudiation of union principles, since both the New York local and the national union then barred principals from membership. Linville's letter of application criticized principals who lacked social vision, because they were in a position to implement wide-ranging reform.[32] It seems that he was quite ready to abandon union leadership for a higher-paying career as a school administrator which would allow him to pursue reform, untrammeled by the mundane material concerns of teachers. Principals were less vulnerable to teachers' interests than teachers' union leaders.

Unsuccessful in his attempt for a principalship, Linville later took an alternate route towards personal improvement: he became a paid, full-time union leader. In 1921, he resigned from teaching in order to assume a union post paid for by contributions and pledges from union members.[33] The similarity between his actions and those of Strachan should be noted. Of course, this comparison should not obscure the considerable differences between Linville and Strachan and

105

their respective organizations. Strachan's astute rise to a prominent position in the New York school hierarchy, as well as her willingness to cooperate with any potential allies in pursuing equal pay, mark her as one of those supervisors whom Linville despised as political appointees devoid of educational merit. For her part, Strachan dismissed both the league and the union as vehicles for Linville and not for teachers.[34] The split between the IAWT and the Teachers' Union, present since the Teachers' League was formed in 1913, widened and deepened during World War I and its aftermath.

When America entered the war, Strachan and the IAWT and Linville and the union responded in radically different ways. Strachan called for preparedness in the schools and criticized high-school teachers and their students for not planning for the war effort. She advocated closing one high school because only a few of its students volunteered for military training, and she criticized foreign-born teachers who had not become naturalized citizens. A month after her views were printed, the IAWT announced that it was forming the Interborough League for War Service and linking its activity in war work with that of the National League for Women's Service. Strachan was elected president of the new group and pledged its help in taking a military census of New York City.[35] In contrast, Linville and his union refused to be stampeded into what he thought was patriotic war hysteria. As already mentioned, the union defended three pacifist members who were attacked for their beliefs by both school officials and other teachers. While not mentioning the IAWT by name, Linville referred to a report on the three pacifist teachers whom the union defended as having been written by "one of the teachers organizations that contains the worst of the reactionaries," a description that certainly characterized his view of Strachan and her membership. He further linked the report to the IAWT when he noted that it came from a group which "has taken particular pains to attack my own career for some years back." He also voiced his personal

106

opinion of Strachan in a letter to Margaret Haley in early 1919. Enclosing an article critical of Ella Flagg Young, Linville attributed it to Grace Strachan and remarked that her authorship alone was enough to make him suspicious of the criticism, though he did not know the details of Young's career.[36]

Strachan's prowar stance was closer to that of most unionists, and most teachers, than Linville's. Linville persisted in defending pacifist teachers, even after Charles Stillman, president of the AFT, apprised him of the serious damage it had done to the union cause; Linville went so far as to condemn the official AFL position of vigorous support for the American war effort. He complained that the labor organization was "largely a movement to maintain a shortsighted group of labor leaders in office" and indicated his personal desire to lead labor out of the hands of Samuel Gompers and his conservative programs.[37]

Strachan's conservative, pragmatic approach appealed to labor on issues besides the war, and in any case, her lobbying experience meant that she was familiar to the state labor hierarchy, whose own primary task was state legislative activity. In 1919, Linville wrote to the president of the New York State Federation of Labor objecting to that organization's backing of a Strachan-supported salary bill instead of one proposed and pushed by the teachers' union. Irvin Yellowitz has characterized organized labor in New York during this period as dominated by the business unionism of the AFL. The state labor federation, responsive to conservative upstate locals, shared more ideologically with Strachan than Linville.[38]

Taken at an abstract intellectual level, the penchant of Linville and his union for advocating reform, both educational and sociopolitical, has a definite appeal. It is particularly attractive when contrasted to the opportunism and rather crass political maneuvering of Grace Strachan. Yet, if we are to understand the teachers' organization movement as it developed in this period, we must recognize that Stra-

107

chan's group was more powerful, more effective, and closer to the views of most teachers than the union. An organization such as Linville's, which chose political and educational reform over service to rank-and-file teachers, seems doomed to ineffectiveness. Linville, when confronted with choices between his ideological desires and the interests of his constituents, seemed usually to choose the former, and thus also chose not to follow a course which might have made his organization considerably more effective. The fact that we know a good bit about Linville's union tells us more about the New York intellectual climate, which has encouraged ideological fighting on the left throughout the twentieth century, than it does about New York's teachers and their organizations. Strachan's group was closer to the realities of teachers' organizational life. Membership in the New York union remained low until the rise of a tough, pragmatic trade unionism under Albert Shanker in the early 1960s. In New York, as elsewhere, a teachers' union could count on significant membership only when it decided to begin its program with the needs of the members. Henry Linville never learned that lesson.

We are now ready to evaluate the several local organizations and leaders discussed in this and the two preceding chapters. The economic motive predominated in the three large organizations, the APSTA, the CTF, and the IAWT. The organization which lacked a consistent salary orientation, the Teachers' League, was not nearly as successful in attaining the allegiance of a significant number of teachers.

The Atlanta and Chicago organizations consistently favored traditional seniority principles in their pursuit of higher salary scales, while the New York groups vacillated on the seniority issue. Henry Linville's league frequently criticized high-school principals as lacking in merit, an indication that for this group experience was not the only criterion of competence. Linville himself, however, paid allegiance to the principle of experience when he cited his years in the schools as one measure of his fitness for the post of high-school principal. The IAWT sought equality for women at all steps of the existing scale, thereby acknowledging the validity of experience as the criterion of merit. Grace Strachan's rapid rise to a district superintendency suggests that she used political connections rather than experience as her primary personal qualification for advancement. This rise, however, took place after the administrative reform of the city schools in the 1890s, an indication that while the reform may have neutralized experience, it did not eliminate politics in the schools.

The leaderships of the four organizations, though different in several ways, were similar in that each effectively controlled the members in a way that encouraged organizational survival. Maintenance of the organization has to be a prime objective of any leader, no matter what his or her personal beliefs; without the organization, no programs or goals can be met. In the CTF, IAWT, and Teachers' League, leadership was concentrated in the hands of one or two individuals who differed significantly in their own political beliefs and educational ideals. Margaret Haley was a tough-minded reformer, Henry Linville a visionary socialist, and Grace Strachan a conservative opportunist. However, they shared an ambition which drove them to work extremely hard for their organizations and to dominate them so that they pursued the leaders' goals. In each case, leadership became a route out of the classroom. Haley and Linville were paid officers, able to work full-time for their own and their organization's goals, while Strachan, a district superintendent, had considerable autonomy and control over her own working hours, which enabled her to pursue her personal and organizational goals with equal vigor.

The APSTA, on the other hand, had a series of leaders, no one of whom dominated the organization, but all of whom participated in association affairs over a long period. The net result in Atlanta was not very different from that in the other three organizations. The Atlanta leaders were usually high-school teachers, elementary-school principals, or high-seniority elementary-school teachers who would soon be principals. Leadership in the Atlanta organization was thus passed around among an elite group of school leaders. In Atlanta, principals had the same job flexibility that Strachan had in New York, enabling them to devote time to organizational duties that rank-and-file teachers did not have. In all cases the leadership kept the organzation under rather firm control and pushed it along the path the leaders chose. None of the organizations could be considered a mass democracy, and each exhibited in its own way some characteristics of a maturing organizational bureaucracy.[39]

Despite their control, however, in each organization the leaders also had to respond to the desires and concerns of their members. In the APSTA, the CTF, and the IAWT, those concerns were primarily economic. The members of these organizations tended to be conservative or traditional on political and educational issues. The opposition to the political reform of centralization by teachers in Chicago, New York, and elsewhere seems to be paralleled by the antipathy to political and educational reform exhibited by the Atlanta teachers. In Chicago and New York, where reform was more a part of the climate than it was in Atlanta, teachers could be persuaded by their leaders to support political reforms such as women's suffrage, but only if the reforms were related to the teachers' major economic goals and shaped to fit their more traditional political and social beliefs.

In the next two chapters, the focus will shift away from local teachers' organizations to national teachers' groups. Nevertheless, similarities between the local situations and the national organizations appear. Economic concerns, organizational continuity, and the conservatism of most teachers affected both local and national organizations of teachers.

5

Teachers in the National Education
Association, 1899–1922

In 1857, ten state teachers' associations joined to establish a National Teachers' Association (NTA), the group which eventually became the National Education Association (NEA). The NTA's major objective was to upgrade teaching to a profession, but it had little success in achieving this rather nebulous goal in its early years. In 1870, the NTA became the NEA by becoming an umbrella organization within which four departments—Normal Schools, Higher Education, Superintendence, and Elementary Education—were affiliated. This coalition drifted along for the next fifteen or so years, meeting annually to discuss items of interest to members of the various departments. The object of professionalizing teaching, though still present rhetorically, seems to have become lost in a variety of other concerns. In 1884, the NEA took another step in organizational development when its entrepreneurial president, Thomas Bicknell, used widespread publicity and a financial arrangement with the railroads to improve attendance dramatically at the annual meeting. From this point on, the NEA meeting became the most important single platform in the country from which educational pronouncements were made.[1]

The landmark 1884 meeting also created the National Council of Education. This council, limited to a small number of the nation's leading educators, quickly became the most powerful and respected part of the NEA. It investigated a variety of educational issues, and its members presented the results to each other at annual meetings. This small group of educational leaders also controlled the NEA presidency throughout the rest of the nineteenth century, and, as office-holders, effectively perpetuated their ideas by exercising their right to select the members of the nominating committee that would choose their successors. This leadership made author-itative pronouncements that other educators were expected to follow. The council members no doubt believed that they represented the best minds in American education, but in the words of the official historian of the NEA, the council "stressed opinion rather than fact, judgments rather than evidence, assertion rather than demonstration, and general impressions rather than research." Nonmembers were not convinced of the council's superior wisdom. In the 1890s, some dissident NEA members dubbed the established lead-ership the "old guard" and sought to free the association from its stifling control.[2]

This chapter will stress the part that teachers played in the coalition that eventually wrested control of NEA affairs away from the "old guard." Teachers formed a variety of groups alongside of and within the parent NEA in an effort to make it respond to their concerns. Teachers also joined with their sometime adversaries, school administrators, to defeat the old guard and replace it with more modern leadership. Once teachers and administrators had attained this objective, how-ever, they again became adversaries as each tried to use the NEA for its own purposes.[3] This internal battle was waged at the same time the NEA fought with the AFT for teacher members. The consequences of the administrators' victory over teachers within the NEA and the NEA's defeat of the AFT were that teachers were denied an independent voice within American education for over fifty years. Before de-

112

scribing the organizational reform movement within the NEA and teachers' role in it, I will look at the objectives teachers pursued within the NEA and the organizational vehicles they established to pursue their goals.

Throughout the first quarter of the twentieth century, teachers tried to get the NEA to respond to their pleas for adequate salaries and other material benefits. They used the NEA meetings, the only occasion on which teachers from different localities could communicate in person with each other, to extend these contacts into a national teachers' organization meant to prod the NEA into recognizing and responding to their interests. These NEA-related activities were initiated in 1899, when a group led by Margaret Haley and Catherine Goggin founded the National Federation of Grade Teachers. Most of the membership came from urban industrial areas in the East and Midwest: sixty-five from Chicago, twenty-five from New York City, eleven from Saint Paul, Minnesota, and most of the rest from Massachusetts, Ohio, and Wisconsin. These areas also provided the bulk of the membership for the local teachers' associations which were then beginning to form. Haley was elected president of the now renamed National Teachers' Federation (NTF) in 1902, and the group indicated its intent to exercise an influence on the educational leaders by setting its annual meeting to coincide with the NEA's.[4]

The NTF sought to "secure such conditions for teachers that they may give their best efforts to the cause of education." This purpose was elaborated on in a resolution the federation adopted at its 1903 meeting:

> WHEREAS, Demands are continually made on teachers for a higher scholastic and professional attainment; cost of living is steadily increasing with stationary or decreasing salaries, insecure tenure of office, no provision for old age, and conditions generally under which teachers work such that further progress in education demands immediate betterment of these conditions:
> therefore
> RESOLVED, That it is the sense of the Mass Meeting of teachers held

under the auspices of the National Federation of Teachers that the time has come to bring the facts as to these conditions to public attention and to this end that the subjects of Teachers' Salaries, Tenure of Office, and Pensions should be placed on the general program next year.

The hardheaded emphasis on salaries and other benefits that pervaded the NTF's program was also manifested in its organizational structure. Active membership was limited to classroom teachers, in contrast to the NEA's policy of including all educators and lay people interested in education as well. Catherine Goggin explained that organizations whose membership included both supervisors and teachers were unsatisfactory "owing to the difference in point of view and, consequently, in order to secure any of the ends necessary to promoting the welfare of the teaching force it was necessary to create an organization for teachers only."[5]

The federation quickly sought a hearing for its resolution by sending a copy to the NEA. The New York delegation to the NTF reinforced the teachers' request by sending a letter to the NEA Executive Committee requesting a three thousand dollar appropriation for a study of teachers' working conditions throughout the country. The NEA reacted by temporizing. The NEA Committee on Resolutions endorsed the teachers' concerns but cautioned that they should not allow "commercialism or self-seeking [to] shape their actions, or . . . intemperance [to] mark their utterances." The NEA then approved the establishment of a Committee on Teacher Salaries which would investigate the situation.[6]

With this institutionalized foothold in the NEA and the appointments of Goggin and William McAndrew (who had recently addressed the NTF in support of higher salaries) to the committee on salaries, teachers had substantial grounds for optimism. That optimism, however, was soon tempered by the committee's lukewarm performance. Since the so-called old guard controlled a majority of the committee, it frustrated the desire of the teacher-oriented minority for forceful action. Goggin tried to get the committee to close its report with a specific salary recommendation, "but the majority disagreed with me, consequently the report is a volume of statistics, valuable no doubt, but failing in the highest point which so important a committee's report should contain, viz., some recommendation as to how salaries can be made better, real pensions secured, and the position of a teacher made permanent." Margaret Haley shared both Goggin's lack of confidence in the NEA leadership and her disappointment with the committee on salaries. In 1901, Haley had accused old guard mainstay William T. Harris of pontificating about the glories of American schooling while teachers were being woefully mistreated. She also objected to the NEA's failure vigorously to publicize the work of its salary committee, thereby depriving classroom teachers of data that might be useful to them.[7]

Despite their reservations, teachers could take comfort in the fact that the publication of the committee report on salaries was an unprecedented event in the NEA's history. Having achieved this milestone, teachers would wait six years for the next published indication of NEA interest in their working conditions. In 1911, with Ella Flagg Young in the presidency, teachers successfully arranged another NEA committee, which was appointed "to investigate compensation present and deferred, that is salary and pension of the teachers throughout the United States with a view of determining whether teachers' salaries have increased to keep pace with the increas [sic] in the cost of living and increased professional demands made upon teachers." Among its members were Haley of Chicago and Grace Strachan, district superintendent in New York and leader of the IAWT. Both Haley and Strachan spoke favorably of the committee's work at the 1912 convention, and Haley observed, "I believe our first duty is not the expounding of theories, but the finding of better conditions for the people who are trying to improve the conditions under which our teachers work."[8]

When the committee's report was finally published in 1913, however, it contained little of the material that Haley had wished to see incorporated. It sketched an accurate picture of low-salaried teachers who had received few raises while seeing the cost of living increase by 50 percent since 1896. Haley, however, refused to sign the report because it contained little specific useful information. There were no data on actual salaries in a wide range of cities so that "in any city where teachers were struggling to get the board of education to give them better salaries they would be able to know at once in what cities of about the same size better salaries were being paid; that was one of the things boards of education wanted to know whenever teachers ask for an increase in salary—what do cities of the same size in other parts of the United States pay?" Instead, the report contained data on salaries in only four cities, and those figures were inaccurate, drawn from responses to a questionnaire rather than the actual salary records. Haley wanted the NEA leaders to know that she had refused to sign the salary report because the committee had failed seriously to address the concerns of elementary-school teachers, the group which had originated the idea of a commission on salaries.[9]

While this salary committee was working on its report, teachers were establishing two successor organizations to NTF. In 1912, teachers in Minneapolis and Saint Paul sent a letter to other local teachers' groups proposing a new national federation of grade teachers. Since this federation was to be discussed at the 1912 NEA convention in Chicago, the Minnesota teachers sought the cooperation of Haley, Goggin, and their CTF membership. The Chicago teachers responded favorably, and plans were made for the initial meeting of the new group. The specifics proposed for consideration were similar to those teachers had already been pursuing: smaller class size, better pay, more control of school affairs for teachers, and more practical pedagogy. The new group was officially established at the 1912 NEA convention, taking for its name the League of Teacher Associations. Its stated objective was "to bring associations of teachers into relations of mutual assistance and cooperation, to improve the social and economic status of teachers and to promote the best interests of education." Like its predecessor, the NTF, the new league limited membership to teachers, arguing that administrator members "would intimidate grade teachers." President Grace Baldwin of Minneapolis notified teachers throughout the country of the formation of the league and urged them to join the group to help free the teacher, "first by making her economically secure; second, by lightening her work; third, by relieving her of the kind of supervision which tends to make her labor rather to please those in authority, than for the best interest of her pupils."[10]

Baldwin also noted another important event at the 1912 NEA meeting, the initiation of a Department of Classroom Teachers within the NEA, with several league members as active participants. The prime mover in establishing the new department was Margaret Haley. She had delegated league work to other members of her Chicago teachers' group and concentrated her own efforts on institutionalizing a teachers' voice within the NEA. This was no easy task. She first applied for an organizational charter from the NEA Executive Committee but was told that teachers' interests were already being cared for in the existing Department of Elementary Education. Haley responded that that department was dominated by supervisors and administrators; the new department, by representing teachers and their concerns, would be unlike any other in the NEA. It took Haley a complete year to get full approval for her new department, but she finally succeeded.[11]

Thus, by 1912, teachers had managed to establish a second official NEA committee on salaries and two new organizations to serve their interests, one a loose affiliate and the other an integral part of the NEA, all in pursuit of better salaries and working conditions. These efforts would continue for the next few years. The Department of Classroom Teachers also initiated a series of discussions on the issue of teachers' councils, formally organized groups of teachers who were to advise superintendents on school policies. The councils served teachers by providing an antidote to the close and constant supervision which was then being advocated by many school administrators.[12]

The coming of World War I brought a new urgency to teachers' complaints about their remuneration. Teachers who were on a fixed salary were confronted with a cost-of-living increase of 40 percent between 1915 and 1917. The result was an even greater emphasis on salaries in teachers' groups, since issues such as tenure and pensions had little relevance in an era when many teachers were leaving the schools for better-paying jobs elsewhere. The only way to halt the exodus was to make teaching financially more attractive. The NEA responded just as it had responded to earlier concerns: it prepared another committee report.[13]

This committee, however, proved to be somewhat bolder than its predecessors. It proposed organizations at local, state, and national levels as a solution to financial crisis. It also called for leaders to interpret teachers' needs to other organizations which could help the cause: labor groups, chambers of commerce, women's clubs, and political parties. The committee noted the rise of the teachers' union movement, and it advised the NEA to study the unions and be prepared to cooperate with them, perhaps by providing statistical data. As a final warning, the committee added that if the NEA could not solve the salary crisis with its methods of research and publicity, the unions would dominate—as indeed they should. The growth of the AFT indicated that the NEA did not respond immediately: 101 new union locals were formed in 1919 and an additional 42 in 1920.[14] This growth in unionism as an alternative to the NEA, however, eventually was recognized by the NEA leadership, which moved to meet the challenge by streamlining its organizational structure in an effort to increase membership and provide a powerful national voice for all educators' concerns.

Before considering these organizational changes in detail, I will describe the new leadership which, with the help of teachers, wrested control of the NEA from the old guard.

The first successful challenge to the established leadership of the NEA occurred at the 1897 Milwaukee convention. S. Y. Gillan, a Milwaukeean who edited the *Western Journal of Education*, led a fight to alter the selection of the nominating committee from the then current method of presidential appointment to that of election by state membership caucuses. Margaret Haley was not actively involved in Gillan's 1897 campaign, but she knew it existed and was in favor of the reform. Gillan's plan was approved by the membership and remained in effect without challenge until 1903, but in that year the old guard, led by Nicholas Murray Butler, attempted to return to the previous procedure. Haley this time joined Gillan in defending the members' involvement in nominations, and both decried the Butler proposal as undemocratic centralization which would effectively deprive members of their recently won rights. She argued that female teachers, who made up over 90 percent of the membership and paid their proportionate share of the dues, deserved the right to participate in the nomination process. Haley's forceful speech did not endear her to the NEA leadership, which earlier that year had earned her enmity by refusing to cooperate in finding a meeting room for the NTF. Gillan and Haley spoke emotionally, and Haley's raising of the women's issue intensified the heated situation. Another speaker, Carroll Pearse, attempted to deemphasize the sex issue and concentrate on the democratic justice of membership participation. He was evidently successful, since Butler's motion was defeated and the members' role in choosing the nominating committee was both reaffirmed and strengthened.[15]

Haley participated in NEA structural reform to support the major goal of economic improvement. She tied the two together when she urged an Idaho teacher to ensure that a sizable delegation from his state attended the NEA conventions held in the west. Large-scale attendance by teachers at NEA meetings meant large numbers of votes for teachers' interests.

> I believe the N.E.A. should be made the medium for expressing the most urgent needs in education in the United States. I have no doubt in my mind that the most urgent need is better conditions for teachers and that in securing these better conditions teachers are going to realize that connection between the educational and the economic problem and that they will become a powerful factor in the solution of that problem.

Haley continued to pursue improved benefits in the NEA for the next several years. In 1904, she gave a speech at the convention, "Why Teachers Should Organize," in which she again emphasized material problems and showed how solving them was intimately related to more professional concerns. She also continued to cooperate with S. Y. Gillan in opposing the undemocratic actions of the NEA hierarchy. Haley and Gillan both tried to block the adoption of a new federal charter for the NEA which would take power from the members by giving special status and financial responsibility to two groups controlled by the old NEA leadership, the National Council of Education and the board of trustees. Haley feared that financial control by the board of trustees would cut off funding for teacher-oriented measures like the 1905 salary commission report. William T. Harris, a noted leader of the NEA old guard, remarked that the new charter was intended to prevent "mob rule" of the association. The "mob" was composed of teachers who wished to turn the NEA's attention away from discussions of educational issues towards their own job crises. This time, Haley and Gillan failed, and the new charter was approved by the association and later by Congress.[16]

The next venture of Haley and her allies into NEA affairs was much more successful. In 1910, they elected Chicago School Superintendent Ella Flagg Young as the first female president of the NEA. Elementary-school principals in Chicago spearheaded the early efforts on her behalf, with support from the CTF. In April, three months before the convention and the presidential election, Margaret Haley received a letter from Katherine Blake, an officer in the IAWT, offering that group's help in the campaign. Haley, busy with a local school crisis which threatened Young's superintendency, ignored the letter. Two months later, Haley and the Chicago principals sent a flurry of letters to Blake and Grace Strachan, leader of the New York group, apologizing for the delay in responding and urging their cooperation in the campaign. A rumor that Strachan might seek the presidency for herself had finally galvanized the Chicagoans. Blake and Strachan discounted the rumor and agreed to support Young, though they were miffed at the delay in acknowledging their offer to help. A. E. Winship, a noted educational journalist and a Boston resident, also supported Young.[17]

Haley worked vigorously but behind the scenes. She had Winship reserve a hotel room for her under the assumed name of Kate Tehan, fearing that if her efforts were visible Young might lose some votes. Young was not the candidate of the majority of the nominating committee; her name was submitted in a minority report by Katherine Blake. Both Blake and Strachan spoke from the floor for the Young candidacy, Strachan remarking that fourteen thousand members of the IAWT supported Young. Strachan also brushed off as inconsequential charges, which echoed Harris's concern about mob rule, that the women were resorting to political methods. In any case, the women had the votes: Ella Flagg Young was elected by an almost two-to-one majority. The *Boston Post* acknowledged the election as a victory of the insurgents over the old guard, and despite having remained unobtrusive, Haley received the lion's share of the credit for it.[18]

The insurgents won still another victory at the 1910 convention, when Nicholas Murray Butler unsuccessfully sought to remove Carroll Pearse from the board of trustees on tech-

121

nical grounds. Butler was thwarted when Pearse resigned his position and was then quickly reelected by a membership vote from the floor. Pearse and Young continued to serve on the NEA board and battled with Butler and Secretary Irwin Shepard over several matters for the next full year. After much infighting, the insurgents emerged as clear victors. Pearse was elected as Young's successor at the 1911 San Francisco convention, with firm support from the Chicago and New York teachers in attendance. The New Yorkers were rewarded with the election of Katherine Blake as treasurer, though it required the same procedure of minority report and floor vote that had elected Young a year earlier. Blake, President Young, and President-elect Pearse gave the insurgents a majority on the board of trustees and put them in undisputed control of association affairs.[19]

The 1912 convention brought further victories, but it also saw a split develop between the leading elements in the reform movement, the teachers from New York and those from Chicago. The meeting took place in Chicago, and Haley intended to use the heavy vote of the local teachers to win bylaw changes which would ensure forever the voting power of the membership. With the preponderance of votes coming from Chicago teachers and with Pearse in the chair to make crucial parliamentary rulings, Haley's victory seemed assured. Grace Strachan, however, came to the convention with a different goal. She was determined to win the presidency and she expected support from the Chicago teachers whom she had helped in the Young election two years earlier. This help did not materialize. Both Strachan and Katherine Blake claimed on the floor of the convention that they had been double-crossed.[20]

Haley explained her inaction by stressing that her major goal was bylaw changes and that she did not wish to alienate any members who would support these changes by endorsing Strachan's controversial candidacy. Haley had to have had other reasons, however, since the Chicago block of votes could have carried the presidency, just as it had won on the bylaws. Haley hinted at these other reasons when she remarked that Strachan and the New Yorkers were more interested in the spoils of the presidency than in democratic reform which would enfranchise teachers. According to Haley, Strachan intended to use the NEA presidency as a stepping-stone to the superintendency in New York City. Haley was particularly perturbed at Strachan's threat to use political pressure by the mayor of New York on his Chicago counterpart to force Chicago teachers to support her candidacy. Strachan, on the other hand, argued that female teachers' needs would be better served through her own election to the top position in the NEA than through parliamentary reform. Haley preferred direct democracy to the mediation of a friendly leader. Of course, it should also be noted that Haley's own role as a full-time leader of an independent teachers' organization would be threatened if administrators successfully represented teachers. Strachan sought support from female teachers with the same argument she had used two years earlier in her speeches for Mrs. Young, that a woman at the top of the organization was the major objective. Haley was more interested in securing the rights of the ordinary female teachers. In other words, Strachan's drive typified a middle-class feminism which sought leadership, while Haley reflected a populist-oriented feminism which linked the sex issue with tangible objectives such as organizational reform.[21]

Still another feature of the split was Strachan's association with the recently deposed old guard. She refused to repudiate their support for her candidacy, thereby increasing fears that she was more interested in the perquisites of the presidency than in reforming the NEA. A final wedge was a long-standing regional jealousy. The old guard was predominantly eastern, and Strachan was suspect to Midwesterners such as Haley, Pearse, and Gillan.[22] Given all these differences, it is not surprising that the alliance between the New York and Chicago teachers was short-lived, and in the end Strachan lost the election.

Strachan's defeat, the victory on the bylaws, and the establishment of both the League of Teacher Associations and the Department of Classroom Teachers at the 1912 convention testify to Haley's emergence as a powerful voice for the cause of teachers in the NEA. One commentator went so far as to suggest that there was now a new machine in charge of NEA affairs and that it was located in Chicago.[23] This view, however, drastically overestimated Haley's influence. No matter how much power she might command on the convention floor, she could not improve her position by carrying that influence into the executive bodies of the association. Even if she had been disposed to try to penetrate the association hierarchy, she would have had great difficulty. As leader of a local teachers' federation, her first allegiance necessarily was to her membership and their concerns.

The chief individual beneficiary of the insurgent victories of 1910 and 1912 was not Haley, but Carroll G. Pearse. He and his close associate, J. W. Crabtree, would gain effective control of the NEA executive bodies over the next few years. They would continuously court Haley in order to make sure that her influence at conventions would not be exercised in opposition to their own plans. Pearse aided Haley in her own battle with old guard elements on the 1911 salary committee, and Crabtree sought her cooperation in choosing presidential candidates and in heading off Grace Strachan's final attempt for the NEA presidency in 1915. This defeat further embittered Strachan and she resigned from the association. Haley also dropped out of NEA affairs for a few years when she was forced to fight the bitter battle over the Loeb rule.[24]

Left in full control of the NEA by the defeat of the old leadership and the withdrawal of Strachan and Haley from association affairs, Pearse and Crabtree moved to consolidate their control and to increase the national power and influence of the NEA. In pursuit of these goals, in 1915 they appointed a committee to study reorganization of the association. Haley seemingly had little to fear from this committee, since it was chaired by William B. Owen, successor to Ella Flagg Young as head of the Chicago normal school and a friend of the

124

Chicago teachers. By the time the committee completed its work, however, that friendship would be sorely tested. Owen's committee would come up with a plan that would drastically curtail the development of an independent teachers' voice within the association.[25]

A newspaper report spelled out the rationale underlying the committee's plans. The NEA as it stood in 1915 was large and unwieldy, an organization in which "membership is purely accidental." A reorganization plan would systematically structure the teaching profession in an association "really national in extent." The leadership was set on increasing membership to 250,000, and a group of that size would have to be intelligently organized or it would be chaotic. The NEA would follow the organizational model of the American Medical Association, with teachers, like doctors, affiliated with their national organization through a state association. A federation of state education associations had existed alongside the NEA since 1911, and reorganization would blend the state and national organizations, making membership in one a condition for membership in the other. Reorganization also would increase the control that professional educators exercised over educational affairs, and it would decrease the influence of textbook companies and other outsiders in both the NEA and in the schools.[26] The goals which were spelled out were not ones that teachers could take issue with, and so they did not object to the idea at first.

Reorganization was one of a number of changes Pearse and Crabtree pursued in order to make the NEA into a powerful organization in state capitals and in Washington. The prerequisite for success in all these efforts was a greatly increased membership. In 1917, the business office of the association moved to Washington and the NEA appointed Crabtree as its first full-time secretary. World War I provided Pearse and Crabtree a golden opportunity to increase the membership and power of the NEA by linking it to the war effort. They therefore appointed a Commission on the National Emergency to institute and publicize war work in the schools, and this commission became a forum for other ideas, including federal aid and the creation of a separate federal-level Department of Education. Crabtree soon acquired a field secretary, who was to devote his attention to the association's multipronged national program, including questions pertaining to better salaries and improved support for the schools. The NEA leadership was going to great lengths to encourage increased teacher membership. Crabtree courted unionized teachers through NEA cooperation with the AFT on the matter of obtaining federal aid. He also advocated teacher participation in school administration through the teachers' council movement which had originated in the Department of Classroom Teachers shortly after its establishment, but which had been largely ignored by the NEA leadership. In his autobiography, Crabtree remembered that teacher participation was one of the most effective means of enticing teachers to join the NEA. His wide-ranging approaches to increasing membership worked exceptionally well, and the membership grew from eight thousand in 1917 to over fifty thousand in 1920.[27]

This massive increase in membership spurred the reorganization committee to present a plan for altering the conduct of the national meeting. Prior to reorganization, business was conducted at NEA conventions on a town-meeting basis, with each member present having a vote. A large number of new members would mean chaos unless some method were developed to streamline the convention. The Owen committee plan, presented in 1917, recommended a representative, not mass-member, format. Delegates would be elected to attend the national convention by each state association, which would be officially affiliated with the NEA. Members who were not elected delegates could attend the convention but could not vote. The activist teachers who made up the League of Teacher Associations, however, were not concerned with an orderly national meeting; rather they sought to maintain the power that teachers could wield under the old system, when the teachers of the convention city turned out in force and

controlled the vote on association business. A delegate format would dilute this power, as the results of a similar reorganization in the Illinois State Teachers' Association had recently demonstrated. At the Illinois convention, of a total of
167 voting delegates, 135 were county and city superintendents, college presidents and professors, or elementary- and
high-school principals. Only 14 of the 167 voting delegates
were elementary-school teachers. Reorganization would have
a similar disfranchising effect in the NEA.[28]

In 1918 and 1919, teachers in Pittsburgh and Milwaukee,
the convention cities in those years, cooperated with out-of-
town activists (including Margaret Haley) to use their numbers to reject reorganization and maintain the existing format. In 1920, however, the NEA reorganization movement,
spearheaded by Crabtree and Pearse, turned the tables on
the teachers. That meeting was scheduled for Salt Lake City,
a place where teachers listened to their administrative superiors, not their activist peers from far-off places. Utah conservatism presented the reorganizers with a group of teachers
who would use the town-meeting vote to abolish the town-
meeting format. Reorganization was enacted, despite Haley's
vocal objections. The teachers' fear of administrator dominance was intensified by another provision, which called for
naming state superintendents and NEA state officers as ex
officio delegates to future conventions, thereby insuring that
fifty administrator delegates would be added to those who
would be elected by their state associations. Yet the reorganization was not totally insensitive to teacher concerns. Responding to activist city teachers who wished to have their
organizations affiliated directly with the NEA, not indirectly
through an intermediary state association, the reorganization
plan contained a provision for such local affiliation. Reorganizers also attempted to placate Haley. The convention
quickly passed a tenure resolution which she supported after
she was asked to present it herself.[29]

Despite their defeat on reorganization, Haley and her
teacher allies, most notably Ethel Gardner of the Milwaukee

Teachers' Association, chose to stay with the new NEA. Several factors influenced them. The NEA management wanted to retain the teachers and its conciliatory actions at the 1920 convention reflected this desire; Haley had no available alternative, since her organization had been forbidden from affiliating with labor by the Loeb rule; and the union alternative was becoming less viable as postwar fears of communism and industrial open-shop drives stifled union activity throughout the country. Both the Chicago and Milwaukee teachers' associations officially affiliated with the NEA under the new organizational structure in 1921. They sought to reinvigorate the teachers' voice in the NEA through the Department of Classroom Teachers, but they were soon thwarted. In 1922, William Owen, by then president-elect of the NEA, intervened in the presidential election in the Department of Classroom Teachers to insure the defeat of Ethel Gardner and the election of a candidate loyal to the NEA leadership.[30] Thus, by 1922, the promising victories of teachers in the NEA—the recognition of their salary concerns, the election of Ella Flagg Young, and the 1912 change in the bylaws— had been neutralized. The teachers' independent voice had been quelled in the NEA.

The myriad actors and influences in NEA affairs during the early twentieth century present the student of NEA reform and the teachers' role in that reform with an always complex and sometimes baffling situation. Yet close analysis reveals a pattern analogous to that which characterized other areas of American reform in the Progressive Era. A two-stage analysis of progressive political reform developed by David Thelen can be applied to the situation within the NEA. Political progressivism in its early stages (1890s and 1900s) employed a multiclass coalition of citizens united to stop the economic and political outrages perpetuated by trusts and other large corporations.[31] The coalition of insurgents in the NEA (who also were sometimes called progressives) against the autocratic old guard management shows that NEA internal politics reflected issues and forces similar to those which operated in American political life at large. The year 1910 marked the beginning of a second stage of reform, with the coalition of reformers breaking up into subgroups, each of which pursued its own aggrandizement, not the common interest. Ella Flagg Young's victory was a high-water mark in NEA reform, but the subsequent splits among the insurgents, first between Haley and Strachan in 1912 and later between Haley and Pearse in 1920, indicate a further similarity between NEA and political reformers.

A closer look at the ways in which the interests of Haley and Pearse blended and then diverged reveals the ideological and material forces which joined and then split these NEA reformers. As long as the old guard was in power, the insurgents needed only the common goal of ousting the autocrats and shared democratic sentiments to remain united. Once the insurgents gained power, however, each subgroup in the coalition had an opportunity to advocate its particular interests. Haley and Pearse had enough interests in common to keep their coalition in operation until after World War I; Haley's concern for better salaries and working conditions, particularly at the elementary-school level, overlapped with a good portion of Pearse's personal and institutional agenda. Pearse and his closest ally, Crabtree, were Midwesterners of common background and education, the former having been educated at Doan College and the latter at the Peru, Nebraska, state normal school. Each worked his way up from rural teaching posts through higher teaching and administrative jobs to normal school presidencies, Crabtree at River Falls and Pearse at Milwaukee, Wisconsin.[32]

Haley and her membership had much in common with these men and the institutions they headed, since most elementary-school teachers had been educated at normal schools. The commonalities were reinforced by the differences that both teachers and normal school faculties felt between themselves and the university professors and presidents who made up the bulk of both the old guard and a new

129

elite of professors of education which arose in the NEA after 1910. The struggle between university education departments and normal schools over who would train the teachers needed to staff the rapidly expanding high schools gave elementary-school teachers an additional reason to link their own status with that of the normal schools. When a movement to establish junior highs was started, both elementary-school teachers and normal school educators could conceive it as a downward thrust by the new university elite against the democratic institutions of common school and normal school. Crabtree alluded to this concern when he wrote to Haley in 1914 to notify her of the stand taken by the Normal School Department of the NEA affirming normal school rights in elementary- and high-school teacher training. That department also took another stand which was sure to please Haley; it attacked Rockefeller and Carnegie foundation sponsored activities which meddled in school affairs such as teachers' pensions. Haley's antipathy to the large foundations was fueled by her progressive political sentiments and aggravated by the CTF's battle in the 1890s against the recommendations of a school study commission headed by the president of Rockefeller's University of Chicago.[33]

Normal-school educators and elementary-school teachers also shared an antipathy to what they regarded as the pretentious, pseudoscientific, theoretical discourse of both the old guard and the new educational aristocrats. Pearse and Haley emphasized the practical in pedagogy, not the esoteric. Pearse started an educational journal in 1916 as a medium for practicing administrators in which he criticized the elaborate methods of the university-based, foundation-funded school surveyors who painstakingly gathered mountains of data which resulted in findings either useless to or already known by practicing educators. Pearse sought to build the NEA through links between various groups of practitioners, thereby creating a group of working educators, not educational theoreticians. He therefore needed classroom teachers for his organization, and he took several steps to win them

130

over. In 1919, while the reorganization battle was at full pitch, the NEA appointed a Denver classroom teacher who was a former president of the League of Teacher Associations as a full-time staff member. This move obviously was intended to court teachers, since the Denver teacher had earlier that year made a no-nonsense speech on teacher needs to the Department of Superintendence of the NEA. Pearse also frequently commented favorably on pay raises in his journal and, as already mentioned, the movement for higher salaries received a good deal of attention from Crabtree's NEA staff.[34]

Despite the mutual ideological and material interests of normal-school educators and teachers, and despite Pearse's shrewd exploitation of these interests, the alliance between the Haley and Pearse wings of the NEA broke apart over reorganization. Pearse's plan was geared toward modernizing the organization, not preserving teachers' independence. If the NEA reorganization were coupled with the strong nationalization measures Pearse also advocated (federal aid, departmental status for education, and a national university), the association would emerge as a power to be reckoned with on the national scene. Balky teachers could not stand in the way of these plans, and so Pearse pursued reorganization despite their opposition. Haley and the CTF, like most teachers and teachers' organizations, were beset with local problems throughout this period and were not particularly interested in the spoils of nationalization. Haley wished to preserve the NEA as it stood, or at least the teacher voice within it. The split between Pearse and Haley involved an issue of overriding importance, as was indicated by the unexpected alliances both made on the reorganization issue. Haley cooperated with old guard elements who opposed Pearse on reorganization as they had opposed him on many other matters, and Pearse was supported by some of the university educationists who were simultaneously threatening normal schools.[35]

Pearse shared with the university educationists a commitment to hierarchical organization and administrator dominance in both the schools and the NEA. His administrative background as superintendent of the Milwaukee schools and his journal editorship linked him to practicing administrators, while the university educationists' major task of training school administrators firmly anchored them to the interests of their students. Teacher independence was not a primary concern for any administrator, whether he was in a university, a normal school, or a local school system. The linking of the NEA reorganization to unionism, by both Haley and the Pearse group, indicates the primacy of the teacher independence issue for both camps. Haley described reorganization as a vicious antiteacher scheme proposed by those who opposed unionism. She never called Pearse an antiunionist, and his mild and cautious pronouncements on teacher unionism can be contrasted with those of some of his allies. In 1917, before the reorganization battle had heated up, Pearse's journal carried advice about unionism: the best thing for a superintendent to do was not to fight the union but to understand the forces that created it and move to satisfy teacher needs so that a union would not be necessary. Two years later, Pearse commented editorially on the Philadelphia teachers' consideration of whether or not to organize by advocating organization, but not affiliation with labor. This of course meant affiliation with the modernized NEA. His pronouncements, though antiteachers' union, were measured and mild and never contained attacks on the labor movement itself. The existence of more vigorous antiunionism among administrators is not difficult to document, however. In 1922, Pearse's journal contained a ringing attack on unionism as "Bolshevism" by a Texas educational editor. Pearse never went that far in public statements; direct attacks were contrary to his philosophy of unity for all educators within the NEA. Even though Haley opposed Pearse on reorganization, she disassociated him from his more rabid antiunion colleagues. In later years, she would refer to him strictly in

132

terms of their 1910 and 1912 alliance against the old guard, while ignoring altogether their dispute over reorganization.[36]

Yet, had Haley known of Pearse's treatment of the independent union movement at the Milwaukee normal school, she might not have felt so kindly toward him. In response to his faculty's move to organize an AFT local in 1919, Pearse arranged for the firing of the union president. Pearse still chose not to battle publicly with the union, but the finality of his response indicates that privately he shared much with more outspokenly antiunion administrators. The local union president wrote to the AFT office describing Pearse "as an enemy to the [union] movement" whose activities needed to be exposed so that "the teaching profession would become acquainted with his insides as well as his outsides."[37]

Pearse's Milwaukee actions indicate that, despite his caution and his frequent attempts to conciliate teachers, in the final analysis he was reasserting the executive power that the insurgents had seen as evil when exercised by the old guard. Pearse in Milwaukee, like educational administrators throughout the country, was applying the same kind of centralization scheme to the public schools that he and teachers had earlier stood against in the NEA and that teachers had opposed in local school districts since the 1890s. Most superintendents opposed an independent teacher voice in local school districts, and the NEA reorganization scheme effectively removed an independent teachers' voice at the national level. Professional school administrators, educated at colleges and universities, emerged as the major power in American education in this period.[38] The defeat of teachers' power in the NEA was one case among many where teachers lost to the new educational executives. The consequence of reorganization was a large-membership, administrator-dominated NEA which retained that character until the early 1970s.

The American Federation
of Teachers, 1916–1923

The birth of the AFT in April 1916 did not, of course, signal the beginning of the teachers' movement. In the late 1890s and 1900s, teachers in Chicago, Atlanta, New York, and many other cities formed organizations which sought to better working conditions, and some of these organizations affiliated with local labor movents. Others, such as the San Antonio, Texas, teachers in 1902 and the Butte, Montana, teachers in 1911, affiliated directly with the AFL, bypassing local and state labor groups. These associations affiliated largely for symbolic reasons, hoping to strengthen their own cause rather than seeking particular services from the labor federation. The relationship between local teachers and the AFL did not usually last long. The initiative for affiliation, in almost every case, came from the local teachers and not from the labor organization.[1]

During and after World War I, however, the AFL took a much greater interest in organizing schoolteachers. Wartime conditions were good for the AFL; the American economy prospered with industrial orders from the Allies. Employers, at first hesitant to share the fruits of this prosperity with their workers, were forced by a series of successful strikes to raise

wages in many industries. The AFL profited from its involvement in these strikes, as well as from its favorable relationship with the Wilson administration. This relationship improved even more as America entered the war and employers
and the government realized that industrial peace was important to successful prosecution of the war effort. Membership in the AFL reflected these circumstances; it went from
fewer than two million in 1915 to over four million in 1920.[2]
Thus the founding and early growth of the AFT took place
in a climate of growth for all of organized labor.

Viewing the AFT from a national perspective, however,
risks overlooking the fact that in the beginning it was little
more than a federation of locals.[3] Only when an organization
acquires a national office, staff, and a set of national issues
does the national level become important. A truly national
AFT never developed in the early years of the federation.
Although most teachers could have united to support American involvement in World War I, the New York local's reluctance to favor the war hampered the creation of a consensus,
particularly because New Yorkers controlled the AFT magazine, the *American Teacher*. Early AFT history, therefore,
can best be understood as an extension of various local activities and points of view.

The actual founding of the AFT was almost totally a Chicago affair. The antiunion Loeb rule of the Chicago board of
education sought to break two locals of male and female high-
school teachers, as well as Margaret Haley's CTF. These
three organizations, along with one in Gary, Indiana, a city
easily accessible from Chicago, comprised the four founding
locals of the AFT. This coalition formed the AFT primarily
as part of their reaction to the Loeb rule, as the teachers
thereby served notice on the board that they were going to
fight back. On the other hand, since all three of the Chicago
teacher groups, as well as several others in the country, were
already affiliated with the AFL or local and state labor bodies, the national union of teachers was chiefly an extension of
already existing local alliances. Labor leaders in the AFL and

in the Chicago labor movement had been corresponding with each other and with Chicago teachers about the possibility of forming a national union for six months prior to April 1916. The teachers who formed the national union were greatly encouraged by the unfavorable publicity accruing to union opponents from the passing of the Loeb rule and from the unsuccessful attempt of the superintendent and board in Cleveland, Ohio, to fire teachers who contemplated affiliating with labor.[4]

At the first AFT meetings, however, the three Chicago locals clashed over the presidency. The elementary-school teachers from the CTF thought that the chief union office should go to their own Margaret Haley. The high-school teachers objected, arguing that Haley's orientation to local Chicago issues made her unattractive as a national officer. Accounts of this dispute, written by male high-school teachers, state that the CTF delegates were persuaded by the high-school teachers' argument. Persuasion was not really necessary, however, since the high-school teachers controlled a majority of the votes. This majority elected Charles Stillman of the Men Teachers' Federation president of the AFT, an office he continued to hold until 1923. Stillman's willingness to seek national union office may have been related to his own group's relative lack of power in Chicago school affairs. Its small membership meant that it could not compete with the much larger CTF. In the interests of organizational peace and strength, Haley was elected as a national organizer.[5]

Tension between the CTF and the two high-school groups over the election of officers did not disappear, however. It was soon exacerbated by the Chicago school board's action of June 1916, when it refused, the reader will recall, to rehire sixty-eight teachers for the 1916–17 school year. All but one of the sixty-eight worked in elementary schools, and thirty-eight were members of the CTF. (James E. Clarke has speculated that there was only one high-school teacher among those dismissed because the high-school federation officers kept their membership lists at home. Their secrecy contrasted markedly with the CTF, which wielded its political power openly.) For a time, the three unions stood together against board dismissals, staunchly supported by organized labor. On the crucial issue of financial support for the dismissed teachers, however, organized labor treated the locals differently. Contributions solicited from teacher unionists were used to pay the salary of the single high-school teacher while the case wound its way through the courts, but no funds were directed to the CTF to help pay the salaries of its dismissed members. Haley resented this and, when the firings were upheld in the courts in 1917, she must have weighed it as one of a number of factors which caused her to lead her organization out of the labor movement.[6]

The differences between the Chicago elementary- and high-school teachers' organizations were not primarily over matters of goals and tactics. Rather, as in New York, separate salary scales with higher remuneration for high-school teachers put the two groups at odds.[7] The early AFT officers were almost all high-school teachers, and their concerns dominated the organization. There are no documents identifying which of the early locals were for high-school and which were for elementary-school teachers, but a reading of the *American Teacher* and the correspondence to and from the national office indicates that the group usually was run by male high-school teachers. Haley's withdrawal from the AFT in 1917 meant that the one effective voice within the AFT for female elementary-school teachers was gone. Charles Stillman and Freeland Stecker, male high-school teachers from Chicago, would be the most visible and powerful AFT leaders during its early years.

Like most local groups, the AFT eschewed a militant or radical image in order to appeal to those who were suspicious of a teachers' organization tied to labor. Apparently even the teacher unionists were somewhat reluctant to identify with organized labor. According to Freeland Stecker, a lengthy debate occurred at the first AFT meeting as to whether the name of the organization should include "union" or "federation." Stecker claimed that the victory of the "federationists" was unfortunate in that it took something away from the AFT's identification with organized labor. Correspondence between President Gompers of the AFL and President Stillman of the AFT reveals that Gompers himself suggested the title American Federation of Teachers, and Stillman quickly adopted it. Thus the teachers' disapproval of obvious union identification was abetted, though perhaps unwittingly, by Gompers.[8]

Teachers' reluctance to embrace unionism repeatedly forced the AFT to defend its affiliation with organized labor, even to its own members. The issue of strikes caused continual difficulty, since many teachers felt strikes were inappropriate. An early AFT pamphlet devoted to the question "Can Teachers' Unions Be Called Out on Strike?" reassured potential members on several particulars: 1) the AFT had an official no-strike policy; 2) it did not have to recognize strikes by other AFL unions; 3) Gompers had publicly endorsed both these provisions; and 4) affiliation with the AFT would prevent the occurrence of teacher strikes like the one which had recently occurred in Memphis, Tennessee. The AFT argued that teachers' unions, rather than encouraging strikes, helped prevent them by providing teachers the alternative of union representation and lobbying. The AFT repeated its no-strike pledge at each of its conventions and tried to publicize this action widely.[9]

AFT organizing efforts also had to overcome the contention that labor affiliation meant an alliance with only one social class, thereby contradicting the public school's mission of serving all segments of society. The AFT responded that this argument confused means and ends. Affiliation was a voluntary means to organize for achieving certain goals. Organization and affiliation in no way implied that the schools would not serve the total society; in fact, labor's record as a champion of public education indicated that affiliation would enhance the public-service emphasis of its affiliated teachers.

The fact that all these arguments had to be repeated again and again suggests that the AFT was never totally successful in overcoming the antilabor bias of many of its potential constituents.[10]

The AFT advocated a wide variety of political reforms, many of which were favored by its early locals. Following the New York local, the national sought teacher membership on boards of education and a careful use of standardized tests in the schools. It endorsed women's suffrage, the initiative, referendum, and recall, thereby supporting many of Margaret Haley's political reform goals. And on the issue of vocational education, the AFT followed its parent AFL in supporting vocational programs that were a part of the existing public school system and opposing a business-supported plan of vocational education which would have housed the job preparation programs in separate schools controlled by employers.[11] These reform goals, combined with the advocacy of better salaries, pension benefits, and tenure, meant that the AFT was on record as favoring almost every policy advocated by any of its locals.

Again following the example of every local except perhaps New York, the AFT avoided fiery language or calls to the barricades. Proposals were stated calmly and argued carefully. Educational and political reform were advocated not as radical measures, but as ways of democratizing the schools and society, a goal which at least in theory should have had wide appeal to teachers and other citizens. Even at its most militant, the AFT pursued improved benefits and working conditions, as well as higher standards for entry-level teachers, in language which appealed to teachers' desire for occupational respectability. A paragraph from one of the more strident of the AFT statements, "A Call to Action," provides a good example.

Teaching is a Profession, Not a Trade
For generations public school teachers have salved their pride
with this pitiful substitute for adequate remuneration and a position

of influence in the community. They have refused to face the obvious fact that whereas doctors, lawyers, architects, and other professional men can control their hours, the conditions under which they work, and the amount of their fees, teachers, as individuals, have almost no control over these matters so vital to their welfare. The results are that the vast majority of teachers receive a smaller annual wage than unskilled laborers and exert far less influence in their calling and in the community than skilled workers.[12]

Taking its cue again from high-status occupations, the 1919 AFT convention enacted a code of ethics which contained four paragraphs explicating the teachers' ethical obligations to children, the public, other teachers, and the nation. There were frequent allusions to professional standards, professional obligations, the examples of other professions, and so on, all testifying to the AFT's intent to appeal to teachers initially hostile to labor unions. The early success in attracting locals in conservative southern towns like Memphis and Atlanta is a testimony not only to the extremely low salaries in those cities, but also to the care with which the AFT courted these organizations.[13]

The AFT made some of its most militant pronouncements on the topic of supervisory rating of teachers. Judging by this precedent, one might expect the AFT to take a tough stand against accepting principals and other supervisors as members. Once more, however, the organization muted its rhetoric with actions which appealed realistically to the situations and aspirations of members. Though the original AFT constitution excluded principals and supervisors from membership, within two years that provision was changed to reflect the realities in various localities. In 1918, the convention passed a constitutional amendment allowing locals of principals to be formed in cities or towns where teachers' locals already existed. Shortly after this provision was passed, Samuel Gompers himself invited New York City's principals to join the teachers' union "to further the interests of the teachers of whom you are an important part."[14]

140

Some union members wanted to go even further and allow principals to be members of teachers' locals. As Charles Stillman put it, this was particularly true in "small communities in which, sometimes, the principal is the live wire on which we must rely." But sentiment favoring principals' membership in teacher locals was not limited to the small towns. Henry Linville, leader of the New York local, who himself desired to be a principal, also supported the idea, writing, "It looks now more than ever as if we should have to plan to wipe out the distinction, and take in principals with teachers all thru [sic] the country." Another New York unionist remarked that in the beginning the New Yorkers were divided on the issue; soon, however, those opposed to principals as unionists changed their position because some of the most loyal union members were being promoted and thereby forced to give up their membership.[15]

Throughout the debate, the AFT practice was only to half enforce or simply to ignore the prohibition against principals' membership in locals. President Stillman wrote to the Gary local in January 1918, "in some peculiar situations the national has allowed considerable freedom" in respect to principal and other administrator memberships. Accordingly, in 1919 the Atlanta local was admitted to the AFT, in spite of the fact that its membership reflected heavy participation and some domination by principals. Finally, in 1921 the AFT constitution was formally amended to allow locals to admit principals and other supervisory officers to membership.[16] It would be misleading, however, to conclude that this position meant that the national was recognizing the traditional promotional patterns based on seniority that were then in place in many elementary schools. In fact, with supervisory ratings based on merit, these patterns were in the process of breaking down in most places. What the AFT's twists and turns on the issue meant was that the national was seeking an accommodation on a thorny issue which would enable it to appeal to the largest and most powerful membership it could.

Thus, from the beginning, the AFT pragmatically dealt

141

with issues in the broadest terms. The official pronouncements reflected the organization's best sense of the concerns
of both members and nonmember teachers. Terms such as
"democracy" and "professionalism" were employed to appeal
to as many teachers as possible. Careful handling of the
principal issue indicates that the organization was sensitive
to the close relationships which still obtained between teachers and principals in many locations. Clearly the AFT preferred to exploit those relationships in order to obtain members rather than follow a militant antisupervisor line which
would have alienated many potential members. Though the
AFT's existence as a national organization, divorced by necessity from the immediate financial battles of teachers in
local school districts, gave it some freedom to stray from the
rigid economic emphasis of most of its successful locals, it
never strayed too far, hewing instead to a line which most
local members could comprehend and approve. The national
in its own way was a cautious organization, adopting as best
it could a position attractive to its current and potential
members.

The desire to satisfy all actual and potential teacher unionists which seemed to pervade official AFT documents did not
totally mask some ideological infighting. The major source of
this controversy was the *American Teacher*. Linville's editorial viewpoint was too radical for many AFT members. At
first Stillman tried to mediate between the editor and his
dissident readers, but soon Stillman himself joined the critics.

Early objections to *American Teacher* articles came in February 1917. George Jones, secretary of the high-school teachers' union in Washington, D.C., wrote to Linville (with a copy
to Stillman) that the January and February issues of the
magazine had caused him to become "apprehensive and
alarmed." Jones found a bitter tone in these two issues that
he regarded as unbecoming to a great organization, and he
said that many Washington teachers agreed with him. Both
Linville and Stillman responded. Stillman wrote, "I wish you

had been more definite, citing passages that were offensive to you." He added that the large headlines, which Jones found "glaring," were approved enthusiastically by Chicago teachers. Linville claimed that Chicago's teachers were revolutionary and that Jones's own union had manifested revolutionary principles in its recent salary campaign not unlike those espoused in the *American Teacher*.[17]

To Stillman Linville complained that Jones's letter lacked specific charges and that there was a general lack of support for the journal in the Washington local. Stillman tried to play the role of peacemaker and solicit specific objections; these turned out to be to the use of words like "scab" and others equally "lurid," and to the journal's reliance on unbecoming exhortations. He then wrote to Benjamin Gruenberg, the managing editor, sympathizing with his frustration and explaining that perhaps "we in Chicago and New York had been keyed up by our struggles to a point that we couldn't expect teachers in a great many cities to reach for a year or two." He advised the New Yorkers that the issue would probably cool down, since he had placated Jones, but within a few months Jones had again complained to Stillman that the journal "will appeal to the worst class of teachers, not to the best class, and an American Federation of Teachers will never come to stay, unless led by strong leaders of the country." Jones again failed to identify particular words or passages; likely offenders, however, were the May 1917 article on Prussia or the June front-page headline "The Revolutionist." Whatever the specifics, it is clear that Jones was sure that he spoke for the Washington teachers, and he urged Stillman to do something about Linville's radicalism before it fatally damaged the union.[18]

Apparently Stillman finally joined the ranks of those who thought the magazine an embarassment to the AFT. Late in 1917, Linville informed Stillman that he was supporting a socialist candidate for mayor of New York. The socialist would soon address the New York union and the *American*

143

Teacher was about to publish an article favorable to socialism. Stillman replied angrily, using a recent *American Teacher* article on school politics to illustrate his objections: "The article goes miles beyond most of us when it calmly asserts that 'we find no sign of clear thinking, we find no evidence of constructive programs, except in the socialist movement.' Would it not be about as true to say that any sign of clear thinking automatically reads one out of the socialist party?" Stillman told Linville, "If an interested teacher should read the last issue, he would surely get the impression that we were a strongly socialistic group." The journal was doing the teachers' union a disservice by giving a hearing to the antiwar socialists while the vast majority of teachers in the country supported the war. Stillman reiterated his displeasure a month later, when he wrote to another officer of the New York union that teachers throughout the country had the notion that New York teachers were at best passively loyal to the war effort.[19]

This exchange marked the beginning of a steady deterioration in the relationship between Linville and Stillman. In December 1918, a Chicago high-school teacher wrote to Freeland Stecker, Stillman's colleague in the national union office, about the propagandistic tendencies of the *American Teacher*. She specifically objected to two articles published in November 1918, one on the Industrial Workers of the World and one a strident report of Chicago events. Stillman followed up by trying to exert a veto over the contents of the journal. The December issue was supposed to contain an article on strikes which implied that teachers might strike, and Stillman attempted to edit out the reference before publication. Linville, however, told him that his recommendation for a change did not arrive until after the issue had gone to the printer. Thus relations between the two were further strained.[20]

Linville resented not only Stillman's attempt at censorship, but also his timidity and that of the Washington unionists— particularly L. V. Lampson, who was about to be appointed a full-time AFT organizer. These men exhibited a conservatism that found them "habitually impressed by those of the prospective locals who hunt for something to excuse themselves from joining." Linville was disappointed in Stillman's leadership, his readiness to change his speeches to meet every complaint, his petulance, and his tendency to become dictatorial. The New York editor thought that Stillman, in his efforts to appease conservative teachers, was expressing "what seems to be the most reactionary views, so far as concerns the matter of forging a character for the A.F. of T."[21]

Stillman continued to receive complaints about the *American Teacher* throughout 1919. The financial secretary of a Boston local wrote that his union had been repudiated by teachers who suspected the AFT of being a socialist organization. He went on to state his own belief in unionism as a means of combating socialism, not embracing it as the journal had done in October 1919. The feelings of many members were typified in a series of resolutions passed by the Washington teachers' union in 1919, attacking the *American Teacher* for not representing the "spirit and views of American teachers," but rather those of New Yorkers, who worked in conditions fundamentally different from those in other parts of the country. Washington teachers found the journal virulent and needlessly bitter; it encouraged "subtle opposition to necessary forms of school control," spread "propaganda dangerous to American ideals," and was not "evolutionary" in dealing with governmental or educational reform. It deterred teachers from joining the Washington locals.[22]

The split between Linville's socialist ideology and the pragmatic orientation of most members would continue to widen throughout the early 1920s. It is tempting but probably unwise to take a side in the dispute. Each group had its strength. Linville had a laudably consistent commitment to a set of political and educational principles. Unfortunately for him, many teachers did not agree with those principles. Stillman, bent on building up union membership, necessarily courted teachers with different ideologies. If too many thought the

145

American Teacher radical or unsound, then it was a burden to the movement.[23]

Thus we can see that beneath the calm facade of official pronouncements, a battle was being waged over the nature of the teachers' union. This dispute was never finally resolved, but its very existence testifies both to the diversity of attitudes and orientations within the AFT and to the elected leaders' efforts to overcome this diversity and discipline those whose radicalism made the union controversial.

Organizational controversies also plagued the AFT from its founding. The question of the amount of dues to be charged the teachers was vitally important to both the national and the locals. The AFT office tried to compromise between a figure too onerous on the locals and one which could keep the national solvent. It settled on a monthly dues to locals of ten cents per teacher member, a figure lower than that charged in most unions. Nevertheless, the assessment caused much controversy. The CTF, the largest founding local, objected that the assessment was too high. It agreed to pay only when the AFT (with the help of a subsidy from the AFL) agreed to pay half the salary of Margaret Haley, who would assume the duties of AFT organizer in addition to her responsibility as CTF leader.[24]

When the AFT accepted the *American Teacher* as the official union magazine, the organization's financial problem increased. In July 1916, dues were increased to fifteen cents per member, with five cents of that amount assigned to the journal. The ideological differences between the editor and many of his readers therefore threatened the financial condition of both the journal and the union. Dissident readers would often refuse to subscribe or refuse to pay for issues mailed to them. The journal finally suspended publication in 1921; when membership losses forced the union to trim its expenses, the journal was the obvious place to begin. Publication did not resume until five years later, when the deepest membership losses had ceased and a small upturn was beginning. By that time, however, the *American Teacher* was edited in Chicago and reflected that city's more practical union-ism.[25]

The ideological fighting about the *American Teacher* spilled over into relations between the AFT and its parent AFL. New York unionists, particularly Linville and Abraham Lefkowitz, continued to push for more radical political stands at meetings of both organizations. Lefkowitz got the AFT in trouble with the AFL by opposing that federation's resolution on the League of Nations in 1920. This action caught both Stillman and Samuel Gompers unprepared, and from that point on, Gompers considered both Lefkowitz and the AFT to be unreliable allies. New York unionists further alienated their AFT colleagues by supporting the Brookwood Labor College, a school which provided ideological and political training to unionists. The Chicago pragmatists questioned both the orientation and the legitimacy of Brookwood, since it was not officially affiliated with labor. In 1923, the New Yorkers did not have to launch what had become their annual attempt to remove Stillman from the presidency, because he announced his resignation to return to Chicago's high-school classrooms. A few years later, the other Chicago leader, Free-land Stecker, was ousted from his position as secretary.[26]

Stillman's departure, which might be taken to signal the end of the first period of the AFT's history, was not primarily due to opposition from the New Yorkers. The severe mem-bership loss contributed significantly. But Stillman might have weathered that storm if he had not gotten himself and his union into trouble with Samuel Gompers. The AFT dele-gates to the 1921 AFL convention voted for John L. Lewis in his unsuccessful bid to replace Gompers as president of the AFL. Stillman's reasons are unknown, though he may well have followed the lead of John Fitzpatrick and the Chi-cago Federation of Labor, who vocally supported Lewis. After his victory, Gompers quickly punished the AFT. In 1922, the AFL reduced its financial commitment to the teachers' federation, making it impossible for the AFT to pay the salaries of a full-time president and another full-time

147

organizer. Stillman, too proud to continue in a diminished role, announced to the 1923 AFT convention that he would not be a candidate for reelection.[27]

The end of a full-time presidency and of the paid organizer position hastened the AFT's decline. In New York and Chicago, releasing a teacher for full-time staff work was a landmark in the development of mature union bureaucracies; in Atlanta and in the IAWT in New York, the leadership of administrators who did not have the full-day work commitment of teachers allowed the organizations to function without full-time staff. In all four local cases, the continuity and availability of regular leadership in day-to-day affairs was necessary for organizational prosperity. Had Gompers not cut off the AFT subsidy, the union might not have suffered as badly from the decline in membership, or at least it might have been able to mount some kind of countercampaign. Weakened by a part-time presidency and deprived of its full-time organizer, however, the AFT was stripped of the resources that had helped produce a peak membership of ten thousand in 1920. The result was the end of an effective AFT for almost a decade. The organization remained alive only because of strong participation by some of the well-organized, large-membership locals, such as the one in Atlanta, which maintained its membership and commitment to the AFT despite the decay of the national organization.

It is doubtful that the AFT could have significantly reversed its own decline in any case. The organization was a federation of locals, and a decline in local membership in the early 1920s signaled hard times for the AFT. The strong locals survived because of local circumstances, not because of any contribution or commitment to or from the national organization. In 1920, while the national was still strong, a representative of the Chicago women's high-school union wrote to Secretary Stecker and outlined the reasons for the members' lack of commitment to the national organization. She began by stressing that her group antedated the national and, unlike locals founded by the work of national officials, felt little real relationship to it. She and her colleagues were "a self-centered crowd, to be frank, and we read very little of the good things which are put into our hands." As a result, members were unaware of national programs and much more concerned with local working conditions. She asked that AFT representatives come to a local meeting to publicize the national's work and perhaps generate greater support for it. She added that her local was hampered in increasing its membership by heavy dues for the national office. A high-school teachers' club which competed with the union for members, unencumbered by a national assessment, charged only half the union dues but still had more money for local work; she had heard of similar complaints in other locals. This arrangement left union locals with too little money for the local work that was most important to rank-and-file teachers.[28]

The limits that a local orientation put on union development were illustrated in a Washington teacher's report to the AFT office in 1920. He remarked that the special "problem is maintaining interest in unionism among teachers." For the few years since the union was formed, his local's efforts had been concentrated on campaigning in Congress for a salary increase. "Since that has been partially met teachers seem to be self-satisfied and see no further need for the union." What this teacher and his Chicago counterpart were communicating was that most teachers were not willing to consider the union as anything but a vehicle for the fulfillment of their immediate interests. Since the national organization had little relationship to those interests and since the labor movement itself had direct contact with teachers only at the local level, teachers' commitment to the AFT was extremely tenuous. As the Chicago teacher remarked, "The truth is that the union idea is not more than half understood or accepted by teachers and they are not educated up to the idea of really paying for their union."[29]

Internal disputes and deteriorating relations with the AFL were not the major reasons for the AFT's decline, however. The number of AFT members dropped drastically in the early 1920s because of a strong effort by the rival NEA to enroll teachers. This activity took place simultaneously with the attempt by American business to reverse AFL wartime enrollment gains through the "open shop" or American Plan, which labeled compulsory union shops un-American.

Initially, relations between the AFT and NEA were cordial. In May 1916, one month after the AFT was founded, the New York local arranged with President Stillman to staff an AFT headquarters at the national NEA meeting in New York. AFT spokesmen and other labor leaders appeared on that and subsequent NEA programs. For the next few years, the AFT looked on the NEA meeting as a large gathering of educators in which the union might be able to do good "missionary work" for its cause. A 1918 NEA salary committee referred favorably to the AFT, and the union in turn indicated its commitment to mutual efforts by holding its 1918 convention in Pittsburgh at the same time as the NEA's.[30]

One might label this early NEA-AFT relationship "peaceful coexistence," in contrast with the warfare that developed later. The convivial feelings of these early years were supplemented by actual attempts at organizational cooperation. In 1918, Charles Stillman told Henry Linville that negotiations were then taking place between the two organizations on matters of mutual importance. Linville responded that he would be sure not to jeopardize these negotiations by unduly criticizing the NEA in the *American Teacher*. The organizations cooperated in the campaign for higher salaries and other teacher benefits, as well as in the establishment of a federal department of education. On this latter issue, however, their objectives were not identical. The NEA sought full departmental status for education and cabinet status for the secretary of the new department, which no doubt reflected the drive of Carroll Pearse, J. W. Crabtree, and other NEA administrator-officers for national power for themselves and their organization. The AFT, on the other hand, sought federal aid for teacher salaries as its primary goal. A federal department of education was less important to the union since it would provide no direct payoff for teachers. The union membership also would be less likely to want a powerful Washington presence which would conflict with local ideologies. In 1921, teachers' locals in New Jersey and Rhode Island objected to the AFT's support of federal aid to education, arguing that it would further an undesirable centralization of political power. Furthermore, Catholics in both the AFT and the AFL were afraid that a federal department of education might have unfortunate consequences for Catholic schools.[31]

The relationship between the two organizations began to deteriorate in 1919. AFT membership had grown considerably since 1916, and the NEA moved to meet this challenge. It began to urge higher teacher salaries as the carrot to attract teacher members, while it also urged superintendents to exert pressure on their underlings to join the NEA. In mid-1919, Stillman countermoved by cooperating with the Milwaukee and Chicago teachers to short-circuit a proposed reorganization plan which would have drastically reduced teachers' influence over NEA affairs. When the Milwaukee teachers' association received a bill for legal services rendered on behalf of the teachers, it appealed to the AFT to pay its share of the expenses. Stillman initially demurred, pleading ignorance and noninvolvement. This provoked a four-page letter from the Milwaukee teachers which clearly outlined what had taken place at the NEA convention and specifically described the AFT's role as an ally to the anti-reorganization teachers.[32]

Later in 1919, as the NEA began an open anti-AFT offensive, the union attempted to respond, but in ways which indicated that it stood little chance of winning the battle. In Wisconsin, an AFT member who was elected president of the state teachers' association sought to have his name struck from the union membership rolls in order to make his presidency nonpartisan. Similarly, the Milwaukee Normal School chapter told the AFT organizer, L. V. Lampson, that he should not publicize the union's defense of a member who had been fired. Even though all of the faculty who acted on behalf of that union activist were AFT members, they told Lampson that officially they acted as a committee representing the total faculty. To be identified solely or primarily as union members would be detrimental to both the threatened professor and the union cause, because "our connection with the Federation has been, throughout, one of our chief handicaps in winning the support of nonmembers in the Faculty and in persuading the administrative authorities to consider our arguments." Thus, even on the offense, the AFT reacted defensively to teachers who feared the stigma of belonging to a union.[33] The post-World War I Red scare, the Boston police strike of 1919, and the widely publicized steel strike all operated to tar union members as un-American.

In 1921, when representatives from the Chicago women's high-school union and the Washington, D.C., union wrote to the AFT office seeking guidance in their attempts to cope with the increasingly successful NEA membership campaign, the AFT secretary, Freeland Stecker, responded by first laying out the entire history of the NEA-AFT relationship. He remarked that in the past the AFT had not opposed teacher membership in both organizations, but the NEA's obvious anti-AFT posture necessitated revising that position. Stecker recommended that Washington's teachers not comply with their superintendent's call to join the NEA. However, he also noted that publication of this recommendation might rebound against the AFT and, further, that there might be exceptional cases when joint membership would serve some useful purpose. What Stecker did not say was how the AFT could help its members resist their supervisors' pressure to join the NEA, the AFT essentially was powerless to stop it. The success of the NEA campaign was paralleled by a decline in AFT membership. At the start of the NEA campaign in 1920, the AFT had over ten thousand members; by 1923, membership had plummeted to three thousand.[34]

The AFT could only try to cut its losses and survive. Most often this was accomplished by maintaining the few remaining strong union locals and working in the state education associations to reeducate teachers to the union cause. Reeducation, of course, could not come without unionists cooperating with their nonunion colleagues. Thus the AFT was almost literally forced to go underground for several years. Membership did not regain the 1920 peak until the mid-1930s, when the crisis of the Depression caused many teachers again to consider the union alternative.[35]

The rise of the AFT was related to a prounion climate developed during World War I, and its decline was one result of the business counterattack on unionism in the postwar period, but its early failure must be attributed to the lack of a real raison d'être for the national body. Since the schools were controlled by state laws and funded by local governments, and since teachers' occupational lives depended on those laws and those funds, a national teachers' union was an anomaly. The national education organization that succeeded, the NEA, was not a teachers' organization at all. It primarily served administrators, who had a greater need to improve their profession and who benefited more from the NEA's orientation toward issues. A meaningful national teachers' organization would have to await the development of a specific reason to exist. The Depression might have fueled a powerful national teachers' group, and the rise in AFT membership during the 1930s indicates that at least for a time it did. World War II, however, ended the national movement once again. Conditions favorable to a national teachers' union movement would not come again until the 1960s, when federal financial involvement in education increased and federal judicial and regulatory trends meant that collective bargaining was a realistic goal for most teachers.

7

Organized Teachers and School Superintendents in the Early Twentieth Century

Michael Katz and David Tyack have characterized the organizational changes which took place in the public schools in the late nineteenth century by using the term "bureaucratization," and they have provided generally convincing descriptions and indictments of the process and its consequences. They do not emphasize, however, the internal personnel policies and the various personnel plans superintendents used to harness their teachers to the new organizational arrangements. Though their histories conclude, rightly I believe, that teachers occupy the bottom rungs of the educational hierarchy (along with their students), they do not explain how that came about. This chapter seeks to show how teachers, despite organization, lost power and prerogatives to school superintendents just as they lost power to administrators in the NEA. The classic study of the early twentieth-century superintendency by Raymond Callahan lays bare both the pervasiveness and the limits of the "efficiency" ideology superintendents used to rationalize their own power. In another article, Callahan characterizes as authoritarian the relationships between superintendents and their teachers. This chapter looks for the roots of that authoritarianism and finds them, not just in the attitudes of the superintendents, but also in the proliferation of administrative positions that superintendents encouraged until they were almost completely isolated from their teachers.[1]

Superintendents used one device to bureaucratize employment in the public schools which we have already seen, merit rating of teachers. They used a new surge of rating activity in the late 1910s to institutionalize a number of new supervisory layers in the schools. Organized teachers usually blunted any negative salary consequences from the rating, but they did not succeed in eliminating the rating itself and its use in deciding who would be promoted to the new supervisory positions. Through their devotion to the salary scale, teachers saved experience as the criterion for economic betterment within the occupation of teacher, but they did not stop the proliferation of nonteaching supervisory positions and the use of ratings and other nonseniority criteria (such as university courses and examinations) to decide who would be promoted to supervisor. Perhaps the key change in establishing the new supervision took place when elementary-school principals stopped teaching and became full-time administrators. At that point the principal was no longer the "principal teacher" but had become a kind of mini-superintendent who rated her underlings.[2]

Superintendents successfully combated teacher unionism at the local level while they built their hierarchies, just as the NEA leadership combated the AFT at the national level. Following the lead of the NEA, several "enlightened" city superintendents established councils to try to divert or neutralize their teachers' impulse to unionize. As the threat of unionization subsided in the early 1920s, superintendents felt freer to ignore or even abolish the councils. William McAndrew, superintendent of the Chicago schools through most of the 1920s, typified the new superintendent. His organizational innovations and his abolition of teachers' councils represent the full flowering of the authoritarian superintendency—in a city with teachers' organizations which were powerful, but which nevertheless were unable to combat the changes.

Teachers' organizations in Atlanta and Chicago opposed merit pay because it threatened the seniority system of employment and promotion. In both cities, teachers and their organizations successfully prevented the direct linking of salaries with supervisory ratings. This success, however, did not forestall the continuation of the merit rating system itself and its use in recommending promotions or dismissal. The persistence of the rating process, despite successful opposition to linking it with pay, points to a fact which was either not perceived or was ignored by teachers' organizations: merit rating was used to enhance the administrative differentiation then occurring in city schools. The unwillingness or inability of teachers' organizations to comprehend this administrative expansion left them unprepared to deal with its major outcome, the rise of administrative power over teachers.

The Chicago schools provide a prime arena for studying the administrative differentiation which accompanied the teacher rating system and the seeming acquiescence of teachers' organizations to the process and its consequences. As I have already noted in chapter 1, Chicago teachers successfully overcame Superintendent Cooley's plan to tie salary increases to supervisor's ratings and examination scores. They did not, however, succeed in eliminating the ratings themselves. In 1909, when Ella Flagg Young was installed as superintendent, teachers were content with her move to require that a teacher be informed of her rating before it went to the board of education, but not to abolish the rating system. Teachers' apparent willingness to live with a "properly administered" rating system left them unprepared for the uses to which it might be put by less friendly administrations.

In late 1916, in the midst of the Loeb board's attack on teachers' labor affiliation, the seemingly innocuous rating system became a prime weapon in that struggle. At first, ratings were done only by principals, but in order to overcome the consequences of some principals consistently rating lower than others, the ratings came to be reviewed and "equalized" by the district superintendents. In 1916, these superintendents altered teachers' leaders ratings for reasons other than equity, lowering the marks of CTF leaders. At this time, Superintendent John Shoop, the Loeb board's replacement for the retired Ella Flagg Young, reintroduced secrecy when he failed to inform those whose ratings had been lowered. As on previous occasions, the CTF was able to blunt any immediate consequence—which in this instance would have been dismissal of its members from the teaching force—by compromising with the board and disaffiliating from organized labor. The ranking system itself, however, was not altered, thereby leaving teachers vulnerable to administrative reprisals on later occasions.[3]

Chicago teachers had thus been unable to halt the growth of a three-level hierarchy of raters—principal, district superintendent, and superintendent—which greatly increased the administrators' leverage over the teaching force. The Chicago experience was repeated in many other cities. In Saint Paul, Minnesota, a merit rating system proposed in 1917 called for four levels of raters for elementary-school teachers: principal, supervisors of special subjects (music, art, and penmanship), assistant superintendent, and superintendent. As in Chicago, this system had antiteachers' organization overtones which were noted by the city's elementary-school teachers' federation. That body opposed the merit rating system because of its inherent unfairness, its use as a probable substitute for a salary increase, and its linking to a scheme to break the teachers' federation, but it failed to comment on the complicated administration of a system which put four levels of administrators between the teacher and her final rating.[4] Yet it was this aspect of the system that had the most significant and longest-lasting consequences.

Atlanta's merit rating system was also four-leveled. Principals, supervisors, directors of special subjects, and superintendents all rated the Atlanta elementary-school teachers. Teachers' opposition to rating concentrated on the salary consequences and the secrecy of the system but again ignored the administrative differentiation which it enhanced. Though they successfully eliminated merit pay through a political alliance which forced the removal of the board president and superintendent who had sponsored the system, the rating system itself and the hierarchy of administrators which accompanied it were left intact.[5] One might conclude that teachers in all these cities won the battle over merit pay but lost the war over control of educational affairs to the developing administrative hierarchies and their rating systems.

The experience of rating in Minneapolis, Minnesota, clearly reveals the chasm developing between teachers and administrators. The superintendent, Frank G. Spaulding, proposed a rating system which called for five levels of raters: principals, supervisors, directors of special subjects, assistant superintendent, and superintendent. A committee of school employees studied the proposed rating plan and objected to it on the grounds that administrators "could not possibly know large numbers of teachers well enough to justify definite ratings." As a counterproposal, the committee suggested that ratings of teachers be done by other teachers, "the only ones to be in position to know their associates intimately enough to rate the comparative worth of each one's service." The superintendent's response embodied the hierarchical distinction between teachers and administrators reflected in the merit plan itself. He refused to consider the teacher rater proposal, not on the grounds that teachers were inappropriate as raters, but rather because teachers did not have the time. For teachers to do enough observing to become valid raters, according to the superintendent, they would have to be released from large amounts of teaching time. This would be inefficient. The proper officials to do the rating, those who had the time and responsibility, were the administrators. Rating was part of the administrator's job; teachers who did such time-consuming work would no longer be teachers, but administrators. Merit rating thus was a significant part of the institutionalization of the job hierarchy which was developing in American education and which was separating teachers from their administrative superiors, and yet this fundamental reality was ignored by teachers' organizations.[6]

Superintendents stood at the top of the developing educational hierarchy. They used merit rating and other administrative innovations to create administrative hierarchies which consolidated their own control over the schools and separated them from students and teachers. Teachers' councils were one such innovation many superintendents used, although they may at first seem to run counter to the hierarchical trend. In the 1890s, when councils were first proposed, most superintendents were not receptive to them because councils threatened their authority at a time when it was not well established. After World War I, however, the NEA looked favorably at the idea of councils or teacher participation as part of its drive to keep teachers out of unions, and local superintendents also moved to establish councils during and after the war. Teachers were scarce throughout the war and the immediate postwar years, salaries could not come close to meeting the war-fueled inflation in prices, and workers in private industry unionized with the support of the Wilson administration. Union activity among many city teachers naturally increased. Superintendents were more established in their positions and were willing to have councils that would neutralize teacher unions and simultaneously add another dimension to the growing school organization.

In Minneapolis, for example, Superintendent Spaulding quickly established a council upon his appointment as superintendent, preempting the idea from the teachers' federation. The superintendent's council differed from that desired by the unionists in that it had several levels of administrator members as well as teachers. However, his establishment of the council was enough to satisfy the desires of most teachers,

159

including most unionists. According to the superintendent, the only objections to the plan came from those unionists who were not council members. These teachers argued that their colleagues who had joined the council had been taken by the superintendent "into [his own] camp." Spaulding astutely used the council to siphon off discontent, respond with a flourish to those issues which he could handle, and thwart the development of independent initiatives by teachers. He established a favorable climate by calling for a social affair at the first meeting and announcing at that meeting that a salary increase would soon be forthcoming. Despite this and other moves to encourage development of the councils, however, Spaulding made clear that any power that the members enjoyed, like the power of any part of the school administration, was subsidiary to that of the superintendent. He successfully opposed election of a representative from the council to the board of education on the grounds that such a "representative at meetings of the Board of Education would be in conflict with the established relationship of the Board with the Superintendent." He argued that in effect "it would mean another official with some of the most important responsibilities with which the superintendent is charged." The council functioned, according to Spaulding, to provide advice to the superintendent in the proper chain of command, not independent representation to the board.[7]

The councils as implemented by Spaulding and other superintendents of the World War I era show that these superintendents were only ostensibly more flexible and interested in teachers than their predecessors of the 1890s. They were certainly more effectively in control of their subordinates. The inclusion of principals, supervisors, and other administrators in the council increased administrative control over teachers by providing a forum in which teachers had a voice, but a voice carefully limited by the same hierarchy that existed in the formal administration. Superintendents thus used councils to establish democracy rhetorically at the same time that they substantially strengthened administrative differentiation.

Teachers' organizations never developed a strategy to turn the councils to their advantage. In Chicago for example, although the powerful CTF consistently advocated councils, it seldom forced them to respond to its concerns or to counteract the superintendent's dominance. Councils had been present in some areas of the Chicago school system since the 1890s, and Ella Flagg Young had moved formally to establish them on a systemwide basis during her superintendency, but the councils were not fully implemented until the superintendency of Peter Mortenson in the early 1920s.

Mortenson, an inside choice for the superintendency, came to the position with long experience in the Chicago schools that made him most acceptable to the organized teachers. Even in this climate, however, the council did not aid the teachers' federation. It seemed to serve, instead, as a body for harnessing teachers to the petty problems of the superintendent and other administrators. The elementary-school councils were organized along the lines of the administrative hierarchy of the school system, with local, district, and central council providing advice to the corresponding administrator—principal, assistant superintendent, and superintendent. The minutes of the central council reveal the basically trivial issues which that body considered. Examples of the items taken up include report card revisions, educational efficiency, and physical plant problems such as heating, ventilating, and oiling of the floors. At one typical meeting of the central council, the group acted on four items, three of which were initiated by the superintendent: a measure to prohibit teachers from receiving gifts from pupils and parents, a recommendation to continue having commencement for eighth grade students, and a measure to increase attendance at council meetings. The fourth item, initiated by the membership, seems just as tangential to the real concerns of organized teachers; it was a resolution protesting the *Chicago*

Tribune's award of first place in an Illinois journalism contest to an article about a non-Illinois topic, Washington, D.C.[8]

Occasionally the council did consider significant issues, but not in a fashion which recognized teachers' autonomy. Members of the central council were most interested in the course of study in elementary schools. On one occasion the council passed a resolution that no changes be made in the course of study unless teachers "were adequately and permanently represented on the committee initiating the change." Six months after passage of this resolution, council members reacted to a new history course which was being approved without any teacher involvement by requesting that "the body who makes a course of study be clearly known and defined." The superintendent responded by going on record that teachers should be involved in making the course of study. Four months later, however, teachers were still attempting to implement that recommendation by setting up a complicated committee structure to study the course of study. Later they reflected their frustration over the entire issue by reiterating an eighteen-month-old resolution that "teachers be informed as to who the authors of the course of study are and the reasons for the changes in the various courses." Thus, even in circumstances ostensibly favorable for teachers and their organizations, the councils seemed incapable of independent, meaningful action.[9]

The fate of the Chicago councils under Mortenson's successor, William McAndrew, testifies further to the inability of even organized teachers effectively to counteract the growing administrative power of the superintendent and other administrators.

After extensive formal education, including the completion of a Ph.D. degree at the University of Michigan, William McAndrew spent several years as a high-school teacher and principal in Chicago. In 1889, he was dismissed as principal of Chicago's Hyde Park High School because of a dispute with board members. McAndrew's own account of his dismissal attributed it to his refusal to alter the grades and diploma of the son of a textbook company executive. He depicted himself as an early casualty in the war against educational corruption. He continued to fight that war throughout his career. In his own mind, his accession to the Chicago superintendency thirty-five years after his dismissal constituted his greatest victory.[10]

When he left Chicago, McAndrew first took a small-town superintendency in his home state of Michigan. He quickly moved on to a better position in a prime location for an ambitious schoolman, New York City. He first went to New York as principal of the high school department of the Pratt Institute and then moved on to become principal of a girls' elementary school, organizer and principal of the Girls' Technical High School (later to become under his leadership the Washington Irving High School), and finally associate superintendent of the New York City schools. He rose through the ranks of the system on his reputation as an innovator. At Washington Irving, McAndrew successfully built an institution which offered practical technical education for girls, despite considerable opposition from more traditional schoolmen. He used his reputation as a practical innovator, combined with the offer of superintendencies in other cities, to rise to the number two position in New York's administrative hierarchy.[11]

As associate superintendent, McAndrew became the acknowledged leader of the reform forces in the city schools. One school paper described him as "the ablest schoolman in the city representing the Progressive educational ideas." He led the faction of the city educators which fought to introduce William Wirt's Gary plan into the elementary schools. Wirt's system combined curricular alterations with administrative efficiency, thus appealing both to innovators and to cost-cutters. It called for dividing the school population into two groups of roughly equal size, with one group engaged for half the school day in work in regular classrooms while the other group pursued less traditional activities in workshops, auditorium, and gymnasium. The results were a large dose of nonclassroom work for all pupils and a doubling of the total number of students that could be served by a given number of classrooms. McAndrew championed the Gary plan throughout the bitter battle that was fought over its introduction. He led the reform forces, even though his superior, Superintendent William Maxwell, was on record as suspicious of innovation. Maxwell, nearing the end of his career, was a traditionalist who viewed Wirt's plan as unnecessary and dangerous. As superintendent, he either could not or did not control his subordinates, however, thereby leaving McAndrew free to follow his own ideas. When McAndrew assumed the Chicago superintendency, as we will shortly see, he was not so inclined to tolerate opposition to his ideas.[12]

Teachers, parents, and citizens who shared Maxwell's suspicions of the Gary plan united to thwart its implementation through the mayoral election of 1917. The incumbent mayor, a reformer who supported the Gary plan and a host of other innovations, lost to a Tammany Democrat who linked fears about the negative consequences of "factoryizing" the schools with some antiimmigrant sentiments the mayor had voiced. Many of the parents who feared the Gary changes were immigrants who were suspicious of any alterations in their children's schooling. McAndrew survived the defeat of the Gary plan and remained as associate superintendent and a strong advocate of practical innovations. Five or six years later, however, when that same Tammany candidate was again elected mayor, McAndrew was forced to retire on a pension. Almost immediately, however, he was chosen as superintendent of the Chicago schools.[13]

McAndrew, despite his role in the New York controversy, was chosen as Chicago superintendent with little dispute. He seemed eminently qualified: he had experience in big-city school systems and a reputation as a leading schoolman. Margaret Haley and the CTF had ample reason to expect fair treatment from him. He had worked with Haley on an NEA salary committee in 1905 and had frequently corresponded with the CTF leadership since then. He had gone on record many times as a champion of higher salaries for teachers, had cooperated with Haley and her other allies in the fight to oust the entrenched NEA leadership, and had defended Chicago's teachers' unions in their battle with the Loeb board in 1916. In the midst of the Loeb battle, McAndrew praised Haley's organization in a speech to the AFT, saying that the teachers were being treated with the same political tactics that had driven him from Chicago in the 1880s. He assured his audience that the board's antiunion tactics would backfire and result in more teachers being driven into the union cause. Privately he wrote to Haley that the board's action put "Chicago into the class of the country village where the school trustee struts about glorying in his power over women." McAndrew's continued contact with and vocal support of the teachers' federation, combined with his generally proteacher image in New York, left Chicago teachers unprepared for the way he would treat them as superintendent.[14]

If the Chicago teachers had distinguished between McAndrew's attitudes toward lay school boards and his view of professional school administrators, they might have been more prepared for his conduct as superintendent. McAndrew supported organized teachers when laymen such as board members or politicians opposed them on issues where teacher gains would not threaten the expanding power of school administrators. Thus, for example, he could support teachers' salary campaigns and the teacher-administrator fight to oust the old NEA leadership, but he did not and would not take such a generous view of teachers and their organizations when they clashed with school superintendents over administrative authority. In 1920, McAndrew gave clear evidence of his attitude in an exchange with a New York teacher unionist who had written an article criticizing the rating of teachers by administrators. The unionist saw such rating as ineffective in improving teachers, unnecessary for achieving dismissal of incompetents, and insufficient to determine eligibility for promotion, and maintained that principals and superintendents rated teachers primarily because "it [gave] them a potent means of control" and "a means for compelling uniformity and subservience." McAndrew responded by noting that the point was not whether administrators liked ratings, but rather that ratings were "necessary for the purpose of maintaining and increasing efficiency." He added that administrators were responsible for a large payroll and ratings provided the means for following and supervising the work of the employees on that payroll.[15]

It was this concern for efficiency and administrative responsibility that characterized McAndrew's superintendency. He reorganized the administrative structure of the school system, installing a "line and staff" system to replace unclear authority relationships which had encouraged personal intervention and political manipulation. Rating and close supervision of teachers represented the practical or everyday institutionalization of the new system. He helped develop elaborate "objective" scales by which principals, supervisors, and superintendents evaluated their inferiors. These policies obviously did not make the new superintendent popular with teachers' organizations, but alone they might not have provoked vigorous opposition. They were accompanied, however, by three measures that guaranteed the superintendent the enmity of the CTF and the high-school teachers' unions: abolition of the teachers' councils; the introduction of junior high schools; and a proposal for the "platoon" system of elementary school organization, the Gary plan under a new name.[16]

McAndrew abolished the teachers' councils after they questioned both the junior highs and the platoon schools. He maintained initially that it was inefficient and unnecessary for the councils to meet on school time, as had been traditional in Chicago, and later argued that the councils met "on the call" of the superintendent, a call which he no longer wished to issue. Teachers countered that his actions violated board policy, since the councils were officially incorporated into the rules of the board of education. McAndrew simply ignored this argument, a move that could be expected from one who saw lay boards and obstreperous teachers as obstacles to smooth management. McAndrew eventually so alienated board members, politicians, and citizens that many of them joined the organized teachers in working for his ouster. This was accomplished in the next mayoralty race by electing a machine Democrat who ran on an antisuperintendent platform and removed him from office shortly after the election.[17]

How could a man who appeared to be a friend of organized teachers turn out to be a bitter enemy? A partial answer to this question has already been given: McAndrew supported teachers only when their concerns coincided with those of administrators. This answer needs to be supplemented, however, by additional information about McAndrew and organized teachers in both New York and Chicago before one can fully understand the development of administrator-teachers' organization relationships in the postwar period.

McAndrew's suppression of teachers' councils in Chicago was in direct contrast to positions he had taken while associate superintendent in New York. For example, in 1916 he spoke to the AFT about the necessity of including teachers in school management, remarking that the "management of any school system . . . would be many hundred per cent more intelligent if the intelligence of the whole body were used." One year before this speech, he had included councils as part of his plan for school reform in New York. That more than a decade had passed between his support and opposition is one obvious explanation of McAndrew's reversal on councils. In 1915 and 1916, teachers' unions were forming in many sections of the country; McAndrew's actions resembled those of superintendents like Frank Spaulding in Minneapolis and of the NEA administrators who sought teachers' support in remodeling the association. They represent a tactical interlude of cooperation with teachers that lasted until around 1920. This cooperative attitude was short-lived, however.

One might expect New York's unionized teachers to know that McAndrew was biased against teachers' organization and to pass the knowledge on to Chicago union leaders when he was being considered for the superintendency, particularly because Margaret Haley corresponded frequently with the New York leadership. The negative information was not passed on, however, because of the differences in orientation and composition between the New York teachers' union and the CTF. New York's union leaders shared with McAndrew a general commitment to educational innovation. The union favored the Gary plan, and while opposition from trade unionists and other citizens caused it to abandon that plan, it did so only for tactical reasons. Henry Linville wrote to another teacher, "The good features of the Wirt idea have been queered by the stupid autocracy of the method of compelling everybody to take it whether or not they liked it, teachers and parents alike."[18] Since most of the compulsion came from the mayor's office, rather than from the reformers in the schools, the unionists and McAndrew were not estranged by the fight over the Gary plan. Furthermore, McAndrew and the New York unionists were almost all males associated with the high schools. Given the separation between the largely female elementary-school teaching force and the mostly male high-school teachers in New York, the lack of hostility between the union leaders and the associate superintendent is not surprising. Male high-school teachers had much more in common with school administrators than they did with female elementary-school teachers, given that high-school teachers enjoyed higher salaries and preferred access to promotions.

Unfortunately for Chicago teachers, when Margaret Haley sought advice about McAndrew, she contacted the high-school male unionists, not the female elementary-school teachers who shared the work situation of the CTF membership. (In fact, the enmity that had developed over the NEA presidency between Haley and Grace Strachan effectively closed off the possibility of communication.) New York elementary-school teachers, who had experienced the consequences of McAndrew's innovations, might well have offered

168

a more negative evaluation of his abilities than the high-school unionists. When completing her autobiography in the 1930s, Haley reflected on the advice she had received and recognized why it had been inappropriate. Henry Linville's views were distorted by the fact that "he was a high school teacher and he didn't know what was happening in the elementary school." In retrospect, Haley understood that another reason she had not been warned was that the two major reforms McAndrew pushed—Gary-plan schools and junior high schools—threatened elementary teachers' occupational interests, but did not threaten and occasionally even enhanced the interests of high-school teachers. Platoon schools entailed a drastic reorganization of elementary-school teachers' work lives; junior high schools threatened the jobs of a significant number of elementary-school teachers who were teaching in the seventh and eighth grades and would lose their positions to secondary teachers if junior highs were created.[19]

Upon arriving in Chicago, McAndrew initiated several measures which implied that he was seeking to divide elementary- and high-school teachers. In addition to advocating platoon schools and junior highs, he proposed a new salary scale which carried distinct advantages for high-school teachers and all principals over elementary-school teachers. The CTF quickly opposed the plan, but without support from the men's and women's high-school unions. McAndrew, however, was too zealous in his support of administrative reform effectively to exploit the differences he created. He insisted on close and frequent supervision of all teachers and turned a deaf ear to questions or complaints. His attitude soon cemented an anti-McAndrew coalition of all the teachers' unions with other labor groups and citizens' groups. As in New York, the forces opposed to McAndrew succeeded in ousting him through the election of a machine Democrat mayor who gained office by running his campaign against the superintendent.[20] Again, as in New York, though the teachers' organizations were successful in ousting the prime advocate of bureaucratic school administration, the policies which this administrator created were not eliminated. They were refined and supplemented by similar administrative innovations which resulted in the complex hierarchies that confront teachers today.

Two facts need to be stressed in concluding this account of organized teachers and superintendents: the gap that developed between superintendents and teachers as a result of bureaucratization and the inability of teachers' organizations to deal with the proliferation of administrators and its consequences. In retrospect it seems clear that administrative reforms separated teachers from superintendents to an unprecedented degree. In 1916, while still associate superintendent in New York, William McAndrew published an article, "Criticize in Writing," which contained the rationale for separating the school executive from his employees. McAndrew complained that superintendents were wasting too much of their valuable time adhering to the tradition of being available to hear teachers' complaints in person. He proposed that complaints be put in writing, thereby replacing the personal-political dimension of the old system with a more efficient and less biased procedure. Moreover, superintendents would be freed to attend to their more important executive responsibilities. Eight years later, shortly after assuming the Chicago superintendency and in the midst of installing his line and staff approach to administration, McAndrew specified how the administrative positions would relieve the superintendent of much of the burden of personal communications that hampered his efficiency:

> Other school systems suffer from the tradition that every teacher with a special idea or complaint, every principal, every inventor of a new device, or author of a new book, every friend of an applicant for promotions, should properly take the case to the "head man." Since beginning work here I have, in deference to Chicago usage, received all comers. It is a large price to pay for a reputation of approachability. To each visitor it has been explained that a speci-

fied officer is employed to handle almost every case. Business has slowly adjusted itself to a more expeditious, satisfactory, and less wasteful conduct. A system directly touching 545,929 pupils and paid members must work clumsily on the old village conception of a one-man affair. It must adopt the motto of other big business: "Organize, deputize, supervise."[21]

McAndrew's motto left little room for independent teachers' organizations which would speak meaningfully on school issues. It also seems clear that the interposition of various layers of administrative specialists between teachers and the superintendent effectively created the distance that McAndrew preferred. The failure of teachers' organizations to cope with these administrative initiatives must be counted as a major reason that these organizations emerged from their initial phase of development as ineffective representatives of teachers' interests.

Three features typical of teachers' organizations seem to have prevented them from understanding and countering the bureaucratization of school administration. First, teachers were passive and conservative. As my local case studies and chapter on the AFT illustrate, leadership efforts in areas not related to teachers' immediate economic needs were seldom supported. Given this reality, the head-on conflict with administrators which would have accompanied any attempt to raise the problem of bureaucratization probably would have frightened many teachers out of an organization. Second, teachers were acutely and chronically underpaid. Their constant pursuit of salary, pension, and other benefits left little time for organizations and leaders to challenge the authority of the administration.

Finally, teachers' leaders failed to solve the problem of interlevel relationships within their own organizations, leaving them ill-prepared to deal with the issue elsewhere. This chapter has reiterated the depth of the split between elementary- and high-school teachers. Both the elementary-secondary separation and the split between teachers and principals posed problems for effective organizational activity. In At-

171

lanta, these differences were not acknowledged, leaving the organization free to operate in favor of the high-status groups, the administrators and high-school teachers. In New York and Chicago, the differences were acknowledged by the creation of separate organizations for elementary- and high-school teachers and for elementary- and high-school principals. The separate groups did look out for their members' interests, but not very effectively and not in a way that allowed them to stem the tide of rising authority in the upper administration. Astute superintendents could and did exploit the tension among the various groups of teachers and principals and make sure that no group succeeded in competing with the administrators. In the AFT, the initial exclusion and subsequent inclusion of principals as members, as well as the preponderance of separate high-school and elementary-school locals, testify to that organization's inability to solve the puzzles of the new administrative structures. Superintendents and their allies captured the NEA completely, to the detriment of teachers. In short, no organization I have described in this study dealt with the internal differentiation of schooling in a way that served the interests of teachers independent of their superiors.

Teachers' leaders themselves were ambivalent on the issue of differentiation in the schools and within their organizations. Some were ambitious for administrative appointments and thus could not be expected to challenge the authority which they sought for themselves. Others, like Margaret Haley and Catherine Goggin, streamlined their own organizations. They separated themselves from their members, thereby leaving the organizations poorly armed to battle the consequences of bureaucratization in the schools. The net result of bureaucratization and the teachers' organizations' failure to counteract it was the incorporation of teachers into an occupational hierarchy in which they occupied the bottom rungs. That situation still remains unremedied.

8

Teachers' Organizations:
Past and Present

One major argument of this study, that economic issues dominated teachers' early organizational activities, seems useful as an initial hypothesis in understanding any contemporary teachers' organization. This is not to say that economic benefits are the only goal, or even always the most important goal, of a teachers' organization, but it is to state that the economic factor will usually be dominant. In fact, when the benefits–working conditions emphasis is not present, one may predict that the particular organization will run into trouble from its own membership. My own work on the 1968 statewide Florida teacher walkout bears out this contention. The Florida Education Association leadership eschewed the economic in its rationale for striking, preferring instead to concentrate on the welfare of the schoolchildren and related altruistic and professional explanations for its activities. This left the teaching force unequipped to counter the tough tactics of business and government leaders who opposed the walkout with real economic threats and effective rhetorical statements that "walking out" of classrooms was hardly an indication of professionalism or altruism.[1]

Another of my conclusions, that teachers and their organizations were politically and occupationally traditional, particularly in their devotion to seniority as a basic criterion for promotion and other occupational rewards, also remains important in understanding contemporary teachers' organizations. As I write this conclusion, Atlanta's teachers' organizations are vigorously fighting a board-sponsored attempt to distribute an ever-decreasing number of teaching positions according to the results of competency evaluations and tests, not seniority. Battles like this are likely to be repeated in other cities and states as the demographic trends of the 1980s result in reduced numbers of students in the schools. I have also pointed out how teachers' traditionalism inhibited effective organizational activity in the past. It is likely to do so in the present and in the future. Sociological studies of teachers, such as Willard Waller's, published in 1932, and Dan C. Lortie's, published in 1975, have laid out the occupational factors which contribute to teachers' traditionalism; studies of teachers' own origins also help to explain it. Historians of teachers' organizations, however, have not paid attention to the ways in which this traditionalism influenced organizational programs and activities. This seems to me to be a crucial lack that needs to be remedied if the positions of teachers' organizations on various educational issues are to be understood.[2]

One also may make the general statement that the centralized leadership structure that characterized early teachers' groups is crucial to contemporary groups. Leaders of modern large-membership teachers' unions devote most of their time to complex, time-consuming tasks, such as bargaining and handling grievances, leaving themselves little time and less inclination to allow meaningful member participation in setting goals and planning strategies. Members who disagree with their leaders, in the present as in the past, have limited power to make their disagreements known. Their main recourse seems to be to block or obstruct the leadership in a variety of parliamentary and extraparliamentary ways. If they seek to implement an alternative strategy or program, they have to run for office; if they win, they perhaps face the same separation from the rank-and-file that sparked their own insurgency. Such are the organizational realities in contemporary society.

These generalizations are most important for understanding local teachers' organizations. National-level groups are freer to roam from the immediate economic interests of their members, freer to respond to national political and ideological priorities, and freer to sponsor internal competition for leadership positions. The NEA recently illustrated this freedom when it successfully lobbied for a separate federal Department of Education, one of the dreams of its post-World War I leaders. The options available to state organizations lie somewhere between the extremes of local and national priorities. These state organizations, however, are also the groups least familiar to historians and other educational researchers. The AFT has not had strong state affiliates until the past few years in New York, but this is not and has not been the case for NEA affiliates. Studies of state education associations ought to prove fruitful in adding to our understanding of teachers and their organizations. Of course, these studies must be undertaken with the understanding that state education associations do not necessarily, or even probably, speak for teachers, but rather for their administrative superiors. The attempts of classroom teacher groups to influence "their" organizations are still worthy of attention, however, particularly as in recent years they have become increasingly successful in many states.

Collective bargaining is the most important development in the recent history of most local teachers' organizations; it gives the organization a place in teachers' occupational lives and city or district educational affairs which it may only have dreamed of in the prebargaining era. In terms of this study, however, collective bargaining seems to have emphasized the importance of our generalizations rather than altered them. It enhances, rather than alters, the economic priorities, occupational traditionalism, and centralized leadership of

175

teachers' organizations. Collective bargaining allows the organization to pursue its material goals more aggressively; similarly, it serves the protective traditionalism of teachers. Work rules or economic benefits, once negotiated, seldom will be abolished; rather they will be modified, usually to the teachers' benefit. Finally, the bargaining process creates an even greater need for a centralized teachers' organization with leaders who can effectively represent their teachers and negotiate with the central administration. The bargaining process also imposes a powerful personal discipline on local leaders, making the emergence of politically reformist or radical leaders like Margaret Haley or Henry Linville less and less likely. The evolution of Albert Shanker of New York City from a social democrat and a graduate student in philosophy to a tough-minded, powerful, pragmatic unionist serves as a case in point. His zealous and protective advocacy of teachers' rights has frustrated educational reformers for at least the past ten years. When reform can be reconciled with teacher benefits, however, Shanker and other leaders can be expected to be much more receptive to it.

Collective bargaining has altered local teachers' organizations through its tendency to centralize or consolidate separate organizations. In cities like New York and Chicago, where separate organizations existed for teachers at different grade levels, collective bargaining has meant the merger of the organizations into one group which can negotiate for all teachers on all issues. This development seems to have concealed some variables which are important for understanding teachers and teaching. The different sexual make-up and occupational training of elementary- and secondary-school teachers is more obvious to students of early teachers' organizations than it is to those who look only at contemporary groups. The feminist issue which was extremely significant for Margaret Haley and Grace Strachan and their organizations has not assumed a comparable significance for contemporary teachers' organizations in which female elementary-school teachers are members together with mostly male

176

high-school colleagues. In fact, contemporary feminist teachers might conclude that they are battling the same male dominance within their own organizations that exists in school systems and in the larger society.

Of course, there is another, largely unexplored side to the feminist issue which is worth attention. Sociological studies of contemporary teachers' organizations have documented the preponderance of male high-school teachers in the ranks of teachers' organization militants. Stephen Cole has even partially attributed the rise to power of the United Federation of Teachers in New York City as a reaction of male high-school teachers against the imposition of a single salary scale for teachers in the 1940s.[3] The effect of the single scale, however, has been almost totally neglected by historians of teachers and their organizations, even though the issues of sex and training differences between elementary- and secondary-school teachers are extremely important for a fuller understanding of the teachers' occupation and organizations. It seems reasonable to conclude that the separate organizations which existed prior to and during the adoption of single salary scales, and persevered for a number of years after, represented certain occupational realities in teaching that have since been papered over rather than solved.

The relationships between teachers and administrators also include both the sex issue and differences in occupational training. This study uncovered some stirrings of an independent teachers' consciousness in the early decades of the century that were short-circuited by the NEA reorganization of 1921 and related events in cities and states. High-level administrators then assumed full control of the educational enterprise at local, state, and national levels. Within this hierarchical system, however, there are a number of stories that seem worth exploring. What of the relationship between principals and teachers? We have seen pioneering organized teachers articulate a view of their occupation that heavily emphasized experience over advanced training as the prime criterion for the principalship. How long did it take for the

177

advocates of advanced education to capture the principal-ship, if they ever did, and what was the consequence of the victory of the educated principal for his or her relationship with the teachers? Similar questions come to mind about the relationship between teachers and subject matter supervisors, guidance counselors, and the other administrative specialties that developed in the past fifty or sixty years. And, of course, the sex issue cuts across differences in the qualifications of those who advanced in the school hierarchy and those who were left behind in the classroom.

Questions like these show how the study of teachers' organizations leads one close to the realities of teaching and teachers. The periods and issues that seem minor in an institutional history may turn out to be critically important for the study of the occupation and its practitioners. The records of local teachers' organizations, which are plentiful in many cases, may thus lead historians to new and valuable insights into the nature of twentieth-century American schools.

There is also a wider arena in which studies of teachers and their organizations are significant. Teachers have much in common with other white-collar workers and other public employees, two groups which are expanding and which are prime targets for today's union organizers. Thus, study of teachers' organizations can and should provide clues for understanding work, workers, and workers' organizations in contemporary American society.

Notes

Preface

1. Richard Hofstadter, *The Age of Reform.*
2. On reform coalitions in the Progressive Era, see John D. Buenker, *Urban Liberalism and Progressive Reform*, pp. 217–18.
3. William Edward Eaton, *The American Federation of Teachers, 1916–1961*; Edgar B. Wesley, *NEA*; Philip Taft, *United They Teach*; Celia Lewis Zitron, *The New York City Teachers Union 1916–1964*; Robert L. Reid, "The Professionalization of Public School Teachers"; Joseph W. Newman, "A History of the Atlanta Public School Teachers' Association, Local 89 of the American Federation of Teachers, 1919–1956"; James E. Clarke, "The American Federation of Teachers"; Ralph D. Schmid, "A Study of the Organizational Structure of the National Education Association, 1884–1921"; Lana D. Muraskin, "Professionalism and Radicalism in the New York City Teachers' Union, 1927–1935" (Paper presented to the American Educational Research Association, 1974); David B. Tyack, *The One Best System*; Raymond E. Callahan, *Education and the Cult of Efficiency* and "The History of the Fight to Control Policy in Public Education."

Introduction

1. Robert L. Church, *Education in the United States*, p. 289. The best source on the high school in this period is Edward A. Krug, *The Shaping of the American High School, 1890–1920.*
2. John K. Folger and Charles B. Nam, *Education of the American Population*, pp. 77–78.
3. Ibid., p. 82.
4. Ibid., p. 84.
5. Lotus D. Coffman, *The Social Composition of the Teaching Population*, pp. 55–56, 59, 70–74, quotation p. 65.
6. Ibid., p. 70.

179

7. Ibid., pp. 55, 28–30.
8. Carter Alexander, *Some Present Aspects of the Work of Teachers' Voluntary Associations* [hereafter *Teachers' Voluntary Associations*], pp. 38, 99.
9. Ibid., p. 42; F. W. Hewes, "The Public Schools of the United States," pp. 1017, 1020, 1040–41; G. Stanley Hall, "The Case of the Public Schools," quotations pp. 408, 403.
10. Coffman, *Social Composition*, p. 83; Alexander, *Teachers' Voluntary Associations*, pp. 49, 50, 40.
11. Coffman, *Social Composition*, pp. 39, 84, quotation p. 85. The CTF is described at length in chap. 3 below.
12. Alexander, *Teachers' Voluntary Associations*, pp. 50, 40.
13. Coffman, *Social Composition*, p. 43.
14. Ibid., p. 44.

Chapter 1

1. Hall, "Case of the Public Schools," quotations pp. 408, 407; L. H. Jones, "The Politician and the Public Schools."
2. Diane Ravitch, *The Great School Wars*, pp. 115–19.
3. Joseph M. Rice, "The Public School System of New York City"; Jacob Riis, "The Children of the Poor"; Ravitch, *Great School Wars*, chaps. 12–14.
4. Ravitch, *Great School Wars*, p. 119; *School*, 9 May 1895, p. 285, and 18 Apr. 1895, pp. 262–65. *School*, a paper written for the city's school employees, is the best extant source for teachers' views in this period. It is available at the New York Public Library.
5. David C. Hammack, "The Centralization of New York City's Public School System," p. 92; *School*, 27 Feb. 1896 contains the quoted material.
6. Hammack, "Centralization," pp. 113–47; *School*, 31 Jan. 1895, p. 174, and 7 Mar. 1895, p. 214.
7. Ravitch, *Great School Wars*, p. 115; Rice, "Public School System"; *School*, 11 Apr. 1895, p. 254.
8. Ravitch, *Great School Wars*, p. 120, points out that in the early 1890s teachers joined parents and trustees in opposing a proposal to combine the city's primary schools with grammar schools, because the reorganization would reduce the number of principalships available.
9. *School*, 11 Apr. 1895, p. 254; Ravitch, *Great School Wars*, p. 146.
10. The central board minutes are found in *School*; the quotations are from 7 Feb. 1895, p. 183, and 7 Mar. 1895, p. 215. Atlanta had a similar promotion system; see chap. 2 below.
11. *School*, 4 Apr. 1895, p. 247, 16 May 1895, p. 297, 6 June 1895, p. 321.
12. Ravitch, *Great School Wars*, p. 129, notes Rice's charge that principals were less educated than teachers; *School*, 7 Mar. 1895, p. 214.
13. *Margaret Haley's Bulletin*, 31 Jan. 1928, p. 107. This periodical may be found at the Chicago Historical Society.
14. Hammack, "Centralization," pp. 112, 121–22.
15. "Report of the Sub-Committee on the Organization of City School Systems," *Journal of Addresses and Proceedings of the National Education Association* 34 (1895):375–88 [hereafter *NEA Proceedings*]. For a sketch of Draper, see Tyack, *One Best System*, pp. 130–33. One proposal in the New York plan not found in the Draper plan was an increase in the number of superintendents. While the large enrollment in New York's schools made more district superintendents desirable, cities with fewer students saw no reason to increase the number.

However, reformers agreed in wishing to augment the power of the citywide superintendent. On the New York teachers' view of the shared liabilities of the Butler and Draper reformers, see *School*, 4 Apr. 1895, p. 246.

16. For a biographical sketch of A. B. Hart, see Samuel Eliot Morison, "A Memoir and Estimate of Albert Bushnell Hart." Hart's challange to Draper may be found in *NEA Proceedings*, pp. 391–95, quotation p. 392.

17. *NEA Proceedings*, p. 397. For the debate between Mann and the grammar schoolmasters, see Church, *Education in the United States*, pp. 97–104.

18. The minutes of the Cambridge School Committee are preserved at the committee office, Cambridge, Mass. Relevant material may be found in the minutes for 20 Dec. 1894, 20 Feb. 1896, 13 Mar. 1896, 18 Feb. 1897. At the time Hart's proposal was formally rejected, teachers were engaged in a salary struggle with the committee; however, there is no evidence directly linking the two events. On the salary matter, see the minutes for 17 Dec. 1896.

19. Minutes of the Cambridge School Committee, 16 Mar. 1899.

20. *Report of the Education Commission of the City of Chicago* [hereafter Harper *Report*], pp. xi–xvi.

21. Mary J. Herrick, *The Chicago Schools*, pp. 84–85; Harper *Report*, p. 64.

22. Reid, "Professionalization," pp. 65–67, 86–88.

23. Tyack, *One Best System*, p. 260.

24. Reid, "Professionalization," pp. 53–55, 57.

25. Ibid., pp. 72–75, 119.

26. Ibid., pp. 71, 76, 118, 120.

27. Ibid., pp. 86–87, 118–19, quotation p. 118.

28. For a brilliant discussion of professionalism applied to school affairs in the 1950s, see Myron Lieberman, *Education as a Profession*.

29. On shoemakers' defense of their traditions against the threat of industrialization and its ramifications in school affairs, see Michael B. Katz, *The Irony of Early School Reform*, pp. 80–84; see also Herbert G. Gutman, *Work, Culture, and Society in Industrializing America* and Daniel Nelson, *Manager and Workers*.

30. *NEA Proceedings*, p. 394. Hart, in arguing his case for a teachers' role in school affairs, said, "What makes Yale University the vigorous, pushing, forceful institution that it is? The governors? In part; but chiefly the faculty—that is, the teachers."

31. See John T. McManis, *Ella Flagg Young and a Half Century of the Chicago Public Schools* or Joan K. Smith, *Ella Flagg Young*. The Harper *Report*, pp. 167–68, contains the discussion of councils as proposed by the administrative reformers.

Chapter 2

1. Howard L. Preston, *Automobile Age Atlanta*, p. 10.

2. On the New South and Henry Grady, see C. Vann Woodward, *Origins of the New South, 1877–1913*; population figures are taken from Timothy James Crimmins, "The Crystal Stair," p. 22. See also Herrick, *Chicago Schools*, p. 403; Melvin W. Ecke, *From Ivy Street to Kennedy Center*, pp. 452–53.

3. Alexander, *Teachers' Voluntary Associations*, p. 67.

4. *Atlanta Constitution*, 29 May 1897. The full range of reasons for the board changes is discussed in Philip Noel Racine, "Atlanta's Schools," pp. 54–56. The corporal punishment issue is explored in Charles E. Strickland's unpublished "Parents versus the Schools? The Case of Atlanta, 1872–1897." On the

politically based reward system that developed after reform, see Racine, "Atlanta's Schools," pp. 95–96.

5. *Annual Report of the [Atlanta, Georgia] Board of Education*, vol. 26 (31 Dec. 1897), p. 13. Accounts of the proceedings in these advisory faculties, which would have provided a valuable source for teachers' views, were not entered into the minutes or otherwise preserved.

6. On the Slatons' conservatism, see Racine, "Atlanta's Schools," pp. 101–4; on the reform ideas of new members, particularly Hoke Smith, ibid., pp. 113–14.

7. The achievement of surface changes without altering traditional values or patterns is characteristic of southern reform throughout the Progressive Era; see Woodward, *Origins of the New South*, chap. 14.

8. On the salary situation, see Ecke, *From Ivy Street to Kennedy Center*, p. 69. The seniority system of promotion in the schools predated the salary scale. It may be examined in Walter Bell, compiler, *Personnel Directory 1870–1900* (Atlanta, Ga.: Atlanta Public Schools, 1973).

9. Mary Fant Gilmer, "History, Activities, and Present Status of the Atlanta Public School Teachers' Association," p. 2; Atlanta Public School Teachers' Association, "Minutes of the Board of Directors," Atlanta Education Association Collection, Southern Labor Archives, Georgia State University [hereafter APSTA Minutes], 27 Nov. 1905. The APSTA, forerunner of the Atlanta Education Association, was an exclusively white organization until the 1960s.

10. APSTA Minutes, 2 Dec. 1905. Data on officeholders were obtained from lists of officers found in the association minute books for each year. The employment pattern was described to me by Walter Bell, historian of the Atlanta public schools, in an interview on 27 Aug. 1973.

11. APSTA Minutes, 3 Apr. 1909, 4 Dec. 1909, 7 Oct. 1916; *Atlanta Constitution*, 29 Jan. 1919.

12. APSTA Minutes, 5 Nov. 1910, 6 Nov. 1915, 10 Nov. 1919; "What Has the Association Done for the School Teachers?," *Official Guide and Yearbook 1924–25, Atlanta Public School Teachers' Association*, Atlanta Schools Collection, Atlanta Historical Society.

13. Ecke, *From Ivy Street to Kennedy Center*, p. 82; "Evidence and Proceedings before a Special Committee of Five, Appointed under a Resolution of City Council," June 1918, p. 396. This document was made available to me by Prof. Melvin Ecke, Georgia State University.

14. Gilmer, "History, Activities, and Present Status," pp. 88, 3.

15. APSTA Minutes, 21 Apr. 1906; *Minutes of the Atlanta Board of Education* [hereafter ABE Minutes], 2 June 1906, available at the board office. See also APSTA Minutes, 6 Dec. 1913.

16. *Journal of Labor*, 27 Sept. 1918, 18 Jan. 1919.

17. Ibid., 20 Jan. 1911, 18 Nov. 1910. Gilmer, "History, Activities, and Present Status," p. 40, argues that the association did not participate in the fight for equal pay because not many members were high-school teachers. In an editorial of 12 Feb. 1915, however, the *Journal of Labor* advocated equalization of female and male high-school teachers' salaries followed by equalization of elementary- and high-school salaries.

18. APSTA Minutes, 18 May 1907.

19. *Atlanta Journal*, 18 Dec. 1910; *Journal of Labor*, 18 Nov. 1910, 25 Nov. 1910, 16 Dec. 1910; *Atlanta Journal*, 16 Dec. 1910, 3 Dec. 1910, 15 Jan. 1911, 16 Jan. 1911.

20. On Haley's suit, see chap. 3 below.

21. Ecke, *From Ivy Street to Kennedy Center*, p. 82; *Atlanta Journal*, 15 Jan. 1911, 18 Jan. 1911; APSTA Minutes, 17 Jan. 1911; quotation from the minutes.

22. *Atlanta Journal*, 18 Jan. 1911, 20 Jan. 1911.

23. Ibid., 21 Jan. 1911; APSTA Minutes, 23 Jan. 1911.

24. APSTA Minutes, 1 Apr. 1911, 6 Jan. 1912. The drop in membership is discussed in Gilmer, "History, Activities, and Present Status," p. 25.

25. *Atlanta Journal*, 18 Jan. 1911; *Journal of Labor*, 27 Jan. 1911, 17 Jan. 1911.

26. *Atlanta Constitution*, 25 Feb. 1916; *Journal of Labor*, 22 Jan. 1915. For an extensive account of Guinn, his reforms, and the opposition to them, see Wayne J. Urban, "Progressive Education in the Urban South," pp. 131–41, 201–3.

27. *Atlanta Constitution*, 3 June 1915; "Evidence and Proceedings," p. 53. On Slaton's firing, see ABE Minutes, 5 June 1915.

28. *Atlanta Constitution*, 31 July 1915; *Atlanta Journal*, 7 June 1915; *Atlanta Constitution*, 23 June 1915; *Journal of Labor*, 22 Oct. 1915.

29. *Atlanta Constitution*, 29 May 1918; "Evidence and Proceedings," pp. 18–19, 152–59, 74, quotation p. 19.

30. *Atlanta Constitution*, 10 Aug. 1918, reports passage of the school amendment in the legislature. The paper was full of accounts of the amendment during the first two weeks in August.

31. APSTA Minutes, 6 Oct. 1918, 8 Nov. 1918, 9 Dec. 1918; *Atlanta Constitution*, 10 Dec. 1918, 14 Jan. 1919, 19 Jan. 1919; APSTA Minutes, 22 Jan. 1919; *Atlanta Constitution*, 23 Jan. 1919.

32. *Atlanta Constitution*, 26 Jan. 1919, 18 Feb. 1919, 3 Mar. 1919, 6 Mar. 1919, 24 Apr. 1919, APSTA Minutes, 10 Feb. 1919, 14 Apr. 1919, 6 May 1919, 12 May 1919. For Dykes's election as superintendent, see ABE Minutes, 2 May 1919.

33. APSTA Minutes, 12 May 1919; *Atlanta Constitution*, 3 May 1919, 14 May 1919.

34. APSTA Minutes, 12 May 1919. The material in this section is based on Newman, "History of the Atlanta Public School Teachers' Association."

35. *Journal of Labor*, 17 Feb. 1919, 14 Mar. 1919, 21 Mar. 1919, 12 May 1919; Mary C. Barker, "Events That Organized Local 89, A.F.T.: Background of the Union," Mary Barker Papers, Special Collections, Emory University, Atlanta, Ga., Box 3. It should be noted that Barker, who was selected for the investigating committee as a union opponent, went on to become the AFT national president in the late 1920s. On the AFT no-strike policy, see chap. 6 below.

36. *Journal of Labor*, 16 Jan. 1920, 4 Apr. 1919, 10 July 1921; Barker, "Events That Organized Local 89"; APSTA Minutes, 12 May 1919; *Atlanta Constitution*, 13 May 1919, 14 May 1919.

37. Urban, "Progressive Education in the Urban South," p. 140.

38. Mary C. Barker, "The Atlanta Public School Teachers' Association," Mary Barker Papers, Box 3; *Journal of Labor*, 2 Jan. 1920; *Atlanta Constitution*, 15 Jan. 1920.

Chapter 3

1. Tyack, *One Best System*, pp. 255–68; Joan K. Smith, "Progressivism and the Teacher Union Movement."

2. For example, see a letter of 16 Feb. 1914 to the CTF from Laura Mainster, president of the Baltimore Elementary Teachers' Association, Chicago Teachers' Federation Collection [hereafter CTF Coll.], Chicago Historical Society, Chicago, Ill., Box 42; "The Constitution and Bylaws of the Detroit Teachers Association," 1908, CTF Coll., Box 39.

3. "Inventory of the Chicago Teachers' Federation Papers," p. 7, CTF Coll., Box 1; Reid, "Professionalization," p. 42.
4. Herrick, *Chicago Schools*, pp. 95–96.
5. Reid, "Professionalization," p. 40.
6. Margaret Haley to F. V. Penfield, 16 Feb. 1904, CTF Coll., Box 37; Olive O. Anderson, "The Chicago Teachers' Federation," p. 4; "The Chicago Teachers' Federation," n.d., CTF Coll., Box 35.
7. Anderson, "Chicago Teachers' Federation," pp. 5–6, 33; Reid, "Professionalization," p. 59.
8. "To the Federation Correspondent," 15 Nov. 1904, CTF Coll., Box 38; "To the Teachers of Chicago," 1 Dec. 1908, CTF Coll., Box 39; "What Has the Chicago Teachers' Federation Done for Me?" 28 Sept. 1912, CTF Coll., Box 41; "The Chicago Teachers' Federation Will Hold Three Meetings," Oct. 1914, CTF Coll., Box 42; folder "May-December, 1915," CTF Coll., Box 43, for revenue shortage material; CTF flier, 15 Oct. 1917, CTF Coll., Box 45; CTF flier, 6 June 1918, CTF Coll., Box 46; "Fellow Teacher," 30 Jan. 1920, CTF Coll., Box 47.
9. Warren R. Van Tine, *The Making of the Labor Bureaucrat*, chap. 4.
10. CTF Minutes, 28 Jan. 1899, 4 Feb. 1899, 8 Apr. 1899, 29 Apr. 1899, 27 May 1899, CTF Coll., Box 1; Reid, "Professionalization," pp. 61–62.
11. CTF Minutes, 20 Jan. 1900, 16 May 1903, CTF Coll., Box 1; Reid, "Professionalization," pp. 61–62; CTF Minutes, 22 Feb. 1902, 22 Mar. 1902, 24 Feb. 1900, 13 Feb. 1903, 11 Apr. 1903, 17 Sept. 1904, CTF Coll., Box 1.
12. Reid, "Professionalization," p. 259; Margaret Haley to unknown correspondent, 2 June 1903, CTF Coll., Box 37.
13. Reid, "Professionalization," p. 66.
14. Van Tine, *Making of the Labor Bureaucrat*, pp. 99–101; Margaret A. Haley, "Autobiography," 1935, pp. 384–86, CTF Coll., Box 34 (Haley wrote her autobiography in installments in 1910, 1911, 1934, and 1935; the installment cited is identified by year). Helen Holden to Frances Harden, 22 Mar. 1911, Frances Harden to Helen Holden, 25 Mar. 1911, CTF Coll., Box 41.
15. Smith, "Progressivism and the Teacher Union Movement," pp. 45–52.
16. Tom Johnson to Margaret Haley and Catherine Goggin, 7 Dec. 1901, CTF Coll., Box 36; Herrick, *Chicago Schools*, pp. 107–11, 121.
17. Haley, "Autobiography," 1911, pp. 113, 120–21, CTF Coll., Box 32.
18. Ibid., pp. 128–31; Reid, "Professionalization," pp. 47, 109–42; Herrick, *Chicago Schools*, pp. 116–20; Francis G. Blair to Margaret Haley, n.d. [1914?], Robert C. Moore to Margaret Haley, 6 Oct. 1914, CTF Coll., Box 42. Both Blair and Moore were candidates for the Illinois state superintendency. For involvement in the superintendency in 1920, see CTF Coll., Box 48.
19. Margaret Haley to Edward F. Dunne, 25 Mar. 1913, CTF Coll., Box 41.
20. Reid, "Professionalization," pp. 109–12, 133; Jane Addams, *Twenty Years at Hull House*, p. 331.
21. Robert F. Pearse, "Studies in White Collar Unionism," p. 107.
22. *Chicago Teachers' Federation Bulletin* [hereafter *CTF Bulletin*] 1 (3 Oct. 1902):6; ibid. 3 (13 May 1904):4; Haley, "Autobiography," 1911, CTF Coll., Box 32. *CTF Bulletin* may be found at the Chicago Historical Society.
23. "Important to Teachers," 31 May 1916, CTF Coll., Box 45; *CTF Bulletin* 5 (6 Apr. 1906):4; ibid. 3 (4 Mar. 1904):4–5; ibid. 2 (3 July 1903):12.
24. *CTF Bulletin* 5 (30 Mar. 1906):4; ibid. 2 (30 Oct. 1903):3; ibid. 2 (13 Feb. 1903):6 (quotation); ibid. 3 (13 Dec. 1903):3–5; ibid. 5 (6 Apr. 1906):1–5; ibid. 4 (2 June 1905):5; ibid. 6 (12 Apr. 1907):4 (quotation); ibid. 1 (7 Nov. 1902):2 (quotation); ibid. 4 (9 Dec. 1904):5; ibid. 2 (28 Nov. 1902):6.

25. Margaret Haley [by Catherine Goggin] to Minnie J. Reynolds, 5 Jan. 1914, Mary A. Doyle Brennan to Margaret Haley, 10 Apr. 1914, Mary A. Doyle Brennan to Margaret Haley, 11 Apr. 1914, Eva Pope to Margaret Haley, 7 May 1914, Anna H. Shaw to Margaret Haley, 25 Mar. 1914, CTF Coll., Box 42. Haley's lack of involvement in the 1914 national suffrage battle also may have been related to her satisfaction at the fact that Illinois women had gained state suffrage in 1913. On the advice to a teacher to drop suffrage work, see Mrs. Ricketts Snell to Margaret Haley, 30 July 1904, CTF Coll., Box 38.

26. Margaret Haley to Fidelia Jewett, 3 Jan. 1914, CTF Coll., Box 42; Margaret Haley to Ida L. Fursman, 26 Dec. 1911, CTF Coll., Box 41.

27. Alexander, *Teachers' Voluntary Associations*, p. 94.

28. Haley, "Autobiography," 1911, pp. 113–15, CTF Coll., Box 32; *CTF Bulletin* 2 (4 Oct. 1902):4.

29. Charles E. Merriam, *Chicago*, pp. 125–30, 211–12; Barbara W. Newell, *Chicago and the Labor Movement*, pp. 23–24, 36; Herrick, *Chicago Schools*, p. 107.

30. CTF Minutes, 4 Oct. 1902, 18 Oct. 1902, 8 Nov. 1902, CTF Coll., Box 1; John Fitzpatrick to the Chicago Teachers' Federation, 16 Oct. 1902, printed in the pamphlet *To the Teachers of Chicago*, 1 Dec. 1908, CTF Coll., Box 39; Haley, "Autobiography," 1911, p. 114, CTF Coll., Box 32; CTF Minutes, 8 Nov. 1902, 22 Nov. 1902, 6 Dec. 1902, CTF Coll., Box 1; Reid, "Professionalization," p. 78; Catherine Goggin to Carter Alexander, 27 May 1910, CTF Coll., Box 40.

31. George Creel, "Why Chicago's Teachers Unionized"; Margaret Haley to M. L. Morgan, 10 Oct. 1910, CTF Coll., Box 40.

32. Catherine Goggin to T. J. Creager, 1 Feb. 1906, Catherine Goggin to N. C. O'Connor, 1 Feb. 1906, Margaret Haley to John Fitzpatrick, 28 Mar. 1906, CTF Coll., Box 39.

33. Reid, "Professionalization," pp. 157–68; "Extract of the Stenographic Report of Jacob M. Loeb's Testimony before the Baldwin Senate Commission," 21 July 1915, CTF Coll., Box 43.

34. Reid, "Professionalization," pp. 169–72; Herrick, *Chicago Schools*, p. 131.

35. Reid, "Professionalization," pp. 174–76; "Report of the Executive Board and the Committee on Schools of the Chicago Federation of Labor . . . March 19, 1916, in Regard to the Loeb Rule," CTF Coll., Box 45.

36. Herrick, *Chicago Schools*, pp. 131–37; Reid, "Professionalization," pp. 191–93; "Statement Concerning Tenure Bill Signed by Governor,—Supreme Court Decision under Old Tenure Law,—and Pending Legislation," n.d., CTF Coll., Box 46.

37. For information on affiliation with the Illinois State Federation of Labor, see folder "October, 1915," CTF Coll., Box 43; on the founding of the AFT, see chap. 6 below. The revised constitution substituting "organization" for "federation" is in folder "January-May, 1916," CTF Coll., Box 45. For Haley's note on a possible compromise with Loeb, see Margaret Haley to E. N. Nockels, 19 Sept. 1916, CTF Coll., Box 45.

38. "Report of Conversation with Mrs. Ida L. Fursman," 30 Apr. 1917, "Report of Conversation with Mrs. Prendergast," 30 Apr. 1917, CTF Coll., Box 46; Herrick, *Chicago Schools*, p. 135.

39. "Report of John Fitzpatrick . . . Recommending the Withdrawal of the Chicago Teachers' Federation from the Organized Labor Movement," 20 May 1917, Frances E. Harden to The Honorable the City Council [sic], 21 May 1917, "Excerpts from Regular Board Meeting of Board of Education," 13 June 1917, CTF Coll., Box 46.

40. Herrick, *Chicago Schools*, p. 135; Reid, "Professionalization," pp. 200, 252;

"Inventory of the Chicago Teachers' Federation Papers," p. 4, CTF Coll., Box 1.

41. *Margaret Haley's Bulletin*, 31 Dec. 1926, p. 126.
42. Alexander, *Teachers' Voluntary Associations*, p. 67.

Chapter 4

1. Ibid., p. 97.
2. Willam W. Wattenberg, *On the Educational Front*, pp. 41–66.
3. Taft, *United They Teach*; Zitron, *New York City Teachers Union*.
4. Muraskin, "Professionalism and Radicalism," p. 4; Wattenberg, *On the Educational Front*, pp. 11, 60.
5. Muraskin, "Professionalism and Radicalism"; Stephen Cole, *The Unionization of Teachers*, pp. 11–12.
6. *NEA Proceedings* 48 (1910):34, mentions 14,000 as the IAWT membership figure; *School*, 8 Apr. 1909, p. 286, mentions 12,000, and *School*, 4 Nov. 1908, p. 75, mentions 13,000.
7. Grace Strachan, *Equal Pay for Equal Work* is an account of the equal-pay movement up to 1910; the highlights of the entire movement, including its 1911 victory, are summarized in Richard Finnegan to Margaret Haley, 19 Aug. 1916, CTF Coll., Box 45.
8. Christine Anne Viggers, "The Importance of the Women Teacher's Organization in the Equal Pay for Teachers Controversy," pp. 57–60.
9. *School*, 13 Dec. 1906, p. 142.
10. Strachan, *Equal Pay for Equal Work*, pp. 16, 17; *School*, 10 Oct. 1907, p. 52.
11. Strachan, *Equal Pay for Equal Work*, p. 569; *School*, 12 Nov. 1907, p. 15.
12. *School*, 10 Oct. 1907, p. 52; ibid., 15 Oct. 1908, p. 53; ibid., 29 Oct. 1908, p. 69; ibid., 12 Nov. 1908, p. 87; ibid. 5 Nov. 1908, pp. 75–76; ibid., 19 Nov. 1908, p. 97. A brief summary of IAWT political activity may be found in Sterling D. Spero, *Government as Employer*, pp. 307–8.
13. Strachan, *Equal Pay for Equal Work*, pp. 204, 256.
14. Ibid., p. 225.
15. *School*, 2 May 1907, p. 317.
16. Ibid., 23 Nov. 1911, p. 30; ibid., 5 Dec. 1912, p. 121; ibid., 20 Feb. 1913, p. 234.
17. Ibid., 16 May 1912, p. 361; ibid., 10 June 1915, p. 10; ibid., 13 Jan. 1910, p. 192; ibid., 27 Feb. 1913, p. 239; ibid., 29 Oct. 1914, p. 77.
18. Ibid., 25 Oct. 1911, p. 90; ibid., 4 Nov. 1909, p. 14; ibid., 28 Oct. 1915, p. 161.
19. Aileen Kraditor, *The Ideas of the Woman Suffrage Movement 1890–1920*, pp. 39–57; Taft, *United They Teach*, p. 13; *School*, 29 Apr. 1909, p. 313; ibid., 23 Dec. 1909, p. 158; Strachan, *Equal Pay for Equal Work*, pp. 303.
20. Strachan, *Equal Pay for Equal Work*, p. 81.
21. *School*, 29 Oct. 1914, p. 77; Kraditor, *Ideas of the Woman Suffrage Movement*, p. 212.
22. Henry Linville to E. E. Slosson 19 Jan. 1913, Henry Linville to Mr. Metcalf, 2 Feb. 1913, Henry R. Linville Collection, The Archives of Labor History and Urban Affairs, Wayne State University, Detroit, Mich. [hereafter Linville Coll.], Box 2.
23. *School*, 6 Mar. 1913, p. 247.
24. Ibid., 13 Mar. 1913, p. 256; "Catechism on the Teachers' Union," American Federation of Teachers Collection, The Archives of Labor History and Urban

Affairs, Wayne State University, Detroit, Mich. [hereafter AFT Coll.], Series 6, Box 3; *School*, 16 Mar. 1916, pp. 371, 372.

25. *School*, 16 Mar. 1916, pp. 371, 372.
26. Charles Stillman to J. E. Mayman, 18 Jan. 1918, Henry Linville to Charles Stillman, 9 Sept. 1918, AFT Coll., Series 6, Box 4.
27. Henry Linville to George J. Jones, 22 Feb. 1917, AFT Coll., Series 6, Box 4.
28. Henry Linville to Leo Blumenfeld, 19 Oct. 1918, Linville Coll., Box 2.
29. Ibid.
30. *School*, 16 Mar. 1916, p. 371; Henry Linville to Rose Schneiderman, 5 Nov. 1918, Linville Coll., Box 2.
31. Henry Linville to Abraham Lefkowitz, 16 Mar. 1916, Linville Coll., Box 2; News Bulletin of the Teachers' Union, vol 3 (1921), nos. 3, 4, 5, AFT Coll., Series 6, Box 4.
32. Henry Linville to the Board of Superintendents, 13 Feb. 1917, AFT Coll., Series 6, Box 4; John L. Tildsey to Henry Linville, 15 Feb. 1917, Linville Coll., Box 3, Henry Linville to Charles Stillman, 25 Feb. 1917, AFT Coll., Series 6, Box 4.
33. Newsletter from Office of Secretary Treasurer, AFT, 17 Jan. 1921, AFT Coll., Series 1, Box 6.
34. *School*, 6 Mar. 1913, p. 247; ibid., 16 Mar. 1916, p. 372.
35. Ibid., 1 Mar. 1917, p. 251; ibid. 26 Apr. 1917, p. 347.
36. Henry Linville to Miss Wilcox, 28 Apr. 1918, Linville Coll., Box 2; Henry Linville to Margaret Haley, 1 Jan. 1919, CTF Coll., Box 47.
37. Henry Linville to Miss Wilcox, 28 Apr. 1918, Linville Coll., Box 2; Charles Stillman to J. E. Mayman, 18 Jan. 1918, AFT Coll., Series 6, Box 4.
38. Henry Linville to James P. Holland, 22 Jan. 1919, Linville Coll., Box 2; Irwin Yellowitz, *Labor and the Progressive Movement in New York State, 1897–1916*, pp. 17, 28.
39. Van Tine, *Making of the Labor Bureaucrat*.

Chapter 5

1. Wesley, *NEA*, chaps. 4, 22.
2. Ibid., chap. 3; quotation p. 265.
3. For a comprehensive look at the NEA in this period, see Schmid, "Study of the Organizational Structure of the National Education Association."
4. "Constitution of the National Federation of Teachers" and "Minutes of the National Teachers' Federation," July 1902, CTF Coll., Box 37.
5. National Teachers' Federation Resolution, 9 July 1903, CTF Coll., Box 38; *NEA Proceedings* 42 (1903):28–29; Catherine Goggin to Cynthia Leet, 8 Dec. 1905, Catherine Goggin to J. Speed Carroll, 5 May 1905, CTF Coll., Box 38.
6. New York Members of the National Education Association to the Executive Committee, National Education Association, 6 July 1903, CTF Coll., Box 37; *NEA Proceedings* 42 (1903):30; "Minutes of the Committee on Salaries, Tenure, and Pensions," 11 Dec. 1903, CTF Coll., Box 37.
7. "Minutes of the Committee on Salaries, Tenure, and Pensions," 11 Dec. 1903, CTF Coll., Box 37; Catherine Goggin to Cynthia Leet, 8 Dec. 1905, CTF Coll., Box 38; Haley, "Autobiography," 1912, pp. 64–71, 99, CTF Coll., Box 32.
8. Margaret Haley to Livy S. Richard, 26 June 1911, CTF Coll., Box 41; *NEA Proceedings* 50 (1912):31–32.
9. *Report of a Committee of the National Education Association on Teachers' Salaries and the Cost of Living*, pp. xi, 16; Margaret Haley to James Ferguson,

11 Feb. 1913, Margaret Haley to Joseph Swain, 13 Feb. 1913, CTF Coll., Box 41.

10. Joint Committee from the Saint Paul Grade Teachers' Federation and the Minneapolis Grade Teachers Association to Grade Teachers, 11 Mar. 1912, Catherine Goggin to Grace Baldwin, 13 Mar. 1912, Grace Baldwin to Ida L. Fursman, 28 Apr. 1912, "Constitution and By Laws of the League of Teachers' Associations," July 1912, "September Communication to Members of the League of Teachers' Associations," CTF Coll., Box 41.

11. Schmid, "Study of the Organizational Structure of the National Education Association," pp. 212–14.

12. National Education Association Committee on Salaries, Tenure, and Pensions, "The Tangible Rewards of Teaching," "A Comparative Study of the Salaries of Teachers and School Officers," "State Pension Systems for Public School Teachers."

13. Committee on Teachers' Salaries, Tenure, and the Cost of Living, *Teachers' Salaries and the Cost of Living* [hereafter cited title only], pp. 9–20.

14. Ibid.; Clarke, "American Federation of Teachers," p. 140.

15. Haley, "Autobiography," 1935, p. 278, CTF Coll., Box 34; Schmid, "Study of the Organizational Structure of the National Education Association," pp. 80–81; *NEA Proceedings* 42 (1903):25–29; Margaret Haley to Irwin Shepard, 4 June 1903, Irwin Shepard to Margaret Haley, 6 June 1903, Edward R. Warren to Margaret Haley, 10 June 1903, CTF Coll., Box 37.

16. Margaret Haley to John Crowley, 31 July 1903, CTF Coll., Box 37; *NEA Proceedings* 43 (1904):145–52; Margaret Haley to S. Y. Gillan, 5 May 1904, S. Y. Gillan to Margaret Haley, 11 May 1904, CTF Coll., Box 38; Haley, "Autobiography," 1911, pp. 99–104, CTF Coll., Box 32; Margaret Haley to S. Y. Gillan, 28 June 1905, S. Y. Gillan to Margaret Haley, 18 June 1904, 8 Oct. 1905, 6 Feb. 1906, CTF Coll., Box 39.

17. Reid, "Professionalization," p. 228; Katherine Blake to Margaret Haley, 19 Apr. 1910, Katherine Blake to Miss Reid [a Chicago principal], 19 Apr. 1910, Margaret Haley to Grace Strachan, 21 June 1910, Katherine Blake to Margaret Haley, 21 June 1910, Catherine Goggin to Elizabeth Allen, 4 May 1910, Catherine Goggin to William McAndrew, 22 June 1910 [the last two letters were inquiries about Strachan mounting a campaign for the presidency of the NEA], CTF Coll., Box 40.

18. Margaret Haley to Frances S. Potter, 12 May 1910, Margaret Haley to A. E. Winship, 28 June 1910, telegram to Kate Tehan, 30 June 1910, CTF Coll., Box 40; *NEA Proceedings* 48 (1910):32–35; clipping, "Mrs. Young Wins: Men Outwitted," *Boston Post*, 8 July 1910, CTF Coll., Box 40.

19. Schmid, "Study of the Organizational Structure of the National Education Association," pp. 185–91. Boxes 40, 41, CTF Coll., are full of clippings and correspondence regarding the fight between Young and the NEA secretary, Shepard. Included are letters to Haley from Gillan, Pearse, Strachan, and Winship, and her replies.

20. Margaret Haley to Misses Cunningham and Rood, 22 June 1912, CTF Coll., Box 41; "The Convention Day by Day," *Journal of Education* 76 (26 July 1912):117–20; "The Chicago Meeting of the N.E.A.," *Western Teacher* 21 (Sept. 1912):1–3; *NEA Proceedings* 50 (1912):34–35, 37–42.

21. Haley, "Autobiography," 1934, pp. 282–91, CTF Coll., Box 34; see also Kraditor, *Ideas of the Woman Suffrage Movement*.

22. *NEA Proceedings* 50 (1912):40; Schmid, "Study of the Organizational Structure of the National Education Association," pp. 191–93, 203–4.

188

23. "Editorial Notes," *Journal of Education* 76 (25 July 1912):115.
24. Carroll Pearse to Margaret Haley, 15 Feb. 1913, 26 Mar. 1913, 11 Dec. 1914, J. W. Crabtree to Margaret Haley, 21 July 1914, 28 Sept. 1914, CTF Coll., Boxes 41, 42; "Miss Strachan Resigns," *New York Times*, 22 Aug. 1915, p. 13.
25. Schmid, "Study of the Organizational Structure of the National Education Association," p. 162; Haley, "Autobiography," 1934, p. 292, CTF Coll., Box 34.
26. *Chicago Tribune*, 25 Aug. 1915; Reid, "Professionalization," p. 234; *Journal of Education* 73 (5 Jan. 1911):16.
27. J. W. Crabtree, *What Counted Most*, pp. 141–47; Crabtree to Active Members, 1 Oct. 1918, Crabtree to Frances Harden, 6 Feb. 1919, CTF Coll., Box 47; Schmid, "Study of the Organizational Structure of the National Education Association," pp. 303–5; Wesley, *NEA*, p. 397.
28. *American School* 3 (Aug. 1917):241; League of Teachers' Associations to Affiliated Clubs, 27 May 1918, CTF Coll., Box 44.
29. Schmid, "Study of the Organizational Structure of the National Education Association," pp. 237, 244–47; Frederick S. Buchanan, "Unpacking of the N.E.A."; *Journal of Education* 92 (19 Aug. 1920):118–20; *American School* 5 (June 1919):164–65; ibid. 6 (July-Aug. 1920):201–2.
30. The CTF charter of affiliation with the NEA, 1 Dec. 1921, is in CTF Coll., Box 49. Box 48 contains letters from the Milwaukee Teachers' Association to the CTF explaining problems with the Milwaukeeans' affiliation. Box 49 contains several affidavits, including one by Margaret Haley, relating to the 1922 officer election in the Department of Classroom Teachers. For an account of this dispute from the side of the NEA loyalists, see Sarah H. Fahey, "History of the Department of Classroom Teachers," p. 177.
31. David Thelen, *Robert M. La Follette and the Insurgent Spirit*, pp. v–vi.
32. Crabtree, *What Counted Most*, p. 7; Louise W. Mears, *The Life and Times of a Midwest Educator: Carroll Gardner Pearse*, chaps. 1, 3.
33. *American School* 2 (May 1916):140–42; ibid. 2 (Dec. 1916):364; ibid. 3 (Feb. 1917):35–37; *Journal of Education* 83 (9 Mar. 1916):256; J. W. Crabtree to Margaret Haley, 21 July 1914, CTF Coll., Box 42.
34. *American School* 2 (Dec. 1916):356–57; ibid. 3 (Jan. 1917):6–7; ibid. 5 (Dec. 1919):356; ibid. 6 (Jan. 1920):3, 5–7, 17.
35. Schmid, "Study of the Organizational Structure of the National Education Association," pp. 237, 248, 253.
36. Reid, "Professionalization," p. 256; *American School* 3 (Mar. 1917): 92; ibid. 8 (Feb. 1922):44; Haley, "Autobiography," 1935, p. 99, CTF Coll., Box 34.
37. Carroll Pearse to L. T. Gould, 30 July 1919, 10 Aug. 1919, L. T. Gould to Freeland Stecker, 4 Sept. 1919, AFT Coll., Series 6, Box 13.
38. On the rise of school administrators, see Callahan, *Education and the Cult of Efficiency*.

Chapter 6

1. Clarke, "American Federation of Teachers," pp. 110–13.
2. Lewis L. Lorwin, *The American Federation of Labor*, pp. 131–35. AFL membership statistics are from Philip Taft, *The A.F. of L. in the Time of Gompers*, pp. 233, 362.
3. For a discussion of the limits of a national perspective on the AFT's history, see Wayne J. Urban, "The Union Label," *Review of Education* 2 (Nov.-Dec.

1976):542–49. Reference in this chapter to the AFT as a "national" in relationship to its locals is technically incorrect. The AFT was and is an international union. I have chosen to refer to it as a national, however, because its activities, like those of the NEA, took place primarily at the national level.

4. Freeland G. Stecker, "The First Ten Years of the American Federation of Teachers," 1950, pp. 3–8, AFT Coll.; Frank Morrison to John Fitzpatrick, 14 Nov. 1915, CTF Coll., Box 43; Stecker, "First Ten Years," p. 11; Clarke, "American Federation of Teachers," pp. 114–20.

5. Stecker, "First Ten Years," p. 11.

6. Clarke, "American Federation of Teachers," pp. 128–31, 135.

7. On the elementary-secondary split in the Chicago teachers' union, see Pearse, "Studies in White Collar Unionism," pp. 139–40.

8. Stecker, "First Ten Years," p. 11; Clarke, "American Federation of Teachers," pp. 121–22; Samuel Gompers to Charles Stillman, 21 Apr. 1916, Charles Stillman to Samuel Gompers, 24 Apr. 1916, CTF Coll., Box 45.

9. "Can Teachers' Unions Be Called Out on Strike?" AFT Coll., Series 1, Box 68; "Platform of the American Federation of Teachers," *Bulletin of the Chicago Federation of Men Teachers and of the Federation of Women Teachers*, Jan. 1917, pp. 2–4, AFT Coll., Series 1, Box 68.

10. "Objections to the Union Movement among Teachers Answered," AFT Coll., Series 1, Box 68.

11. "Platform of the American Federation of Teachers," pp. 2–4.

12. Quoted in Stecker, "First Ten Years," p. 33.

13. "Code of Ethics Adopted by the Fourth Annual Convention of the American Federation of Teachers," AFT Coll., Series 9, Box 1; Stecker, "First Ten Years," p. 19.

14. Henry R. Linville to the Elementary and High School Principals, 4 Nov. 1918, Linville Coll., Box 2; Samuel Gompers, "To the Principals of the Public Schools of New York," AFT Coll., Series 6, Box 4.

15. Charles Stillman to George Jones, 30 Mar. 1918, AFT Coll., Series 6, Box 4; Henry Linville to Charles Stillman, 19 Dec. 1918, Linville Coll., Box 2; J. E. Mayman to Charles Stillman, 30 Mar. 1918, AFT Coll., Series 6, Box 4.

16. Charles Stillman to Anita Bailey, 31 Jan. 1918, AFT Coll., Series 6, Box 2; Charles Stillman to Alice Deas, 16 Jan. 1920, AFT Coll., Series 6, Box 4; *Bulletin of the Office of the Secretary Treasurer*, no. 97 (27 May 1921), p. 1, AFT Coll., Series 1, Box 67.

17. George Jones to Henry Linville, 16 Feb. 1917, Charles Stillman to George Jones, 26 Feb. 1917, Henry Linville to George Jones, 22 Feb. 1917, AFT Coll., Series 6, Box 4.

18. Henry Linville to Charles Stillman, 25 Feb. 1917, Charles Stillman to Benjamin Gruenberg, 21 Mar. 1917, George Jones to Charles Stillman, 28 May 1917, Charles Stillman to George Jones, 3 Oct. 1917, AFT Coll., Series 6, Box 4; *American Teacher* 6 (May 1917); ibid. 6 (June 1917).

19. Charles Stillman to Henry Linville, 1 Dec. 1917, Charles Stillman to J. E. Mayman, 18 Jan. 1918, AFT Coll., Series 6, Box 4; "The Schools in Politics," *American Teacher* 6 (Nov. 1917):127–28.

20. Federation of Women High School Teachers [of Chicago] to Freeland Stecker, 9 Dec. 1918, AFT Coll., Series 6, Box 1; Henry Linville to Miss Wilcox, 5 Jan. 1919, Linville Coll., Box 2.

21. Henry Linville to Miss Wilcox, 5 Jan. 1919, Henry Linville to Mrs. Beers, 9 Feb. 1919, Linville Coll., Box 2.

22. H. P. McLaughlin to Charles Stillman, 16 Oct. 1919, AFT Coll., Series 6, Box

3; "A Perplexed Pedagogue," *American Teacher* 8 (Oct. 1919):183–84; Maude C. Gunther to Freeland Stecker, 14 June 1919, AFT Coll., Series 6, Box 4.

23. *Bulletin of the Office of the Secretary Treasurer*, 19 May 1921, 26 May 1921, AFT Coll., Series 1, Box 67.

24. Alice Graves to Freeland Stecker, 17 Apr. 1916, AFT Coll., Series 6, Box 4; Stecker, "First Ten Years," p. 12.

25. Charles Stillman to [?] Chadwick, 22 July 1916, AFT Coll., Series 6, Box 2; Henry Linville to Charles Stillman, 25 Feb. 1917, Linville Coll., Box 2; Stecker, "First Ten Years," p. 55.

26. Stecker, "First Ten Years," pp. 28–30, 38–43, 31, 61.

27. Ibid., pp. 28, 31. Much of the opposition to Gompers was socialist inspired, and two of the three AFT delegates clearly were against him. Whether Stillman was actively against Gompers is not clear from Stecker's account, but Philip Taft documents the deterioration in the relationship between Gompers and the Chicago Federation of Labor in *A.F. of L. in the Time of Gompers*, pp. 376, 449, 453–55.

28. Lucie W. Allen to Freeland Stecker, 19 Sept. 1920, AFT Coll., Series 6, Box 1.

29. Ibid.; "Armstrong-Dunbar #9," in "To the Presidents and Secretaries of Affiliated Locals," 3 Nov. 1920, AFT Coll., Series 1, Box 67.

30. Charles Stillman to Henry Linville, 20 May 1916, AFT Coll., Series 6, Box 4.

31. Henry Linville to Charles Stillman, 13 Oct. 1918, Linville Coll., Box 2; *Western Teacher* 27 (Nov. 1919):91–92; *Bulletin of the Office of the Secretary Treasurer*, 19 May 1921, AFT Coll., Series 1, Box 67; Marc Karson, *American Labor Unions and Politics, 1900–1918*, chap. 9, discusses the influence of Catholicism on the labor movement and Catholic labor's fear of socialism; on p. 223, Karson notes that Charles Stillman was one of a number of Irish-Catholic union presidents.

32. Nina S. Griffiths [corresponding secretary, Milwaukee Teachers' Association] to Charles Stillman, 7 Oct. 1920, AFT Coll., Series 6, Box 13.

33. L. T. Gould to Freeland Stecker, 10 November 1919, Edith E. White to L. V. Lampson, 18 Feb. 1920, AFT Coll., Series 6, Box 13; Stecker, "First Ten Years," pp. 24, 27.

34. Lucie W. Allen to Freeland Stecker, 3 Jan. 1921, AFT Coll., Series 6, Box 1; Freeland Stecker to Mrs. R. C. Paul, 22 Jan. 1921, AFT Coll., Series 6, Box 4. A chart of AFT membership between 1916 and 1940 may be found in AFT Coll., Series 1, Box 72. Taft, *A.F. of L. in the Time of Gompers*, p. 362, notes a similar drop in AFL membership from over four million in 1920 to three million in 1923.

35. Saint Paul Education Association to Freeland Stecker, 17 Feb. 1922, AFT Coll., Series 6, Box 7; see source cited in n. 34 above for membership figures.

Chapter 7

1. Katz, *Class, Bureaucracy, and Schools*; David B. Tyack, "Bureaucracy and the Common School: The Example of Portland, Oregon, 1851–1913," *American Quarterly* 19 (Fall 1967):475–98; Callahan, *Education and the Cult of Efficiency* and "History of the Fight to Control Policy."

2. Wayne J. Urban, "The Past and the Present in Educational Innovation," pp. 5–17.

3. "To the Editor," n.d. [1904?], CTF Coll., Box 38; to Mr. Buck, 25 Nov. 1916, CTF Coll., Box 44.

4. "The So-Called Merit-System: St. Paul Grade Teachers Federation to the Public," n.d. [1917?] and Isabel Williams to Frances Harden, 18 Nov. 1917, CTF Coll., Box 45.

5. "Evidence and Proceedings," pp. 152–55; Ecke, *From Ivy Street to Kennedy Center*, pp. 120–21.

6. Frank E. Spaulding, *School Superintendent in Action in Five Cities*, pp. 310–18, 501–6, quotations p. 503.

7. Ibid., pp. 472–76, 473, quotations pp. 476, 475.

8. *Reports of the Elementary Teachers' General Council*, passim and 22 Apr. 1923. A copy of the volume is housed in the Regenstein Library, University of Chicago.

9. Ibid., 31 Mar. 1923, 27 Oct. 1923, 22 Dec. 1923, 4 Feb. 1924.

10. William McAndrew, "The Control of the Teacher's Job," p. 103. Margaret Haley discusses McAndrew versus the board, not the circumstances that caused the dispute; see Haley, "Autobiography," 1935, p. 587, CTF Coll., Box 34.

11. *School*, 8 July 1912, pp. 455, 463; ibid., 5 Sept. 1912, p. 4.

12. Ibid., 1 Aug. 1912, p. 464. For a complete account of the Gary plan and the controversy surrounding it, see Ravitch, *Great School Wars*, pp. 195–232. McAndrew's leadership of the "Gary party" is noted in *School*, 16 Aug. 1917, p. 516. *School*, 2 Aug. 1917, p. 499.

13. Haley, "Autobiography," 1935, p. 358, CTF Coll., Box 34.

14. William McAndrew to Catherine Goggin, 12 Jan. 1905, CTF Coll., Box 38; William McAndrew to Margaret Haley, 21 Jan. 1914, CTF Coll., Box 42; To the Program Committee of the Illinois State Teachers' Association, Nov. 1910, CTF Coll., Box 40; Haley, "Autobiography," 1935, pp. 586, 596–97, CTF Coll., Box 34; McAndrew, "Control of the Teacher's Job," pp. 103–4; William McAndrew to Margaret Haley, 12 June 1916, CTF Coll., Box 44. McAndrew and other reform superintendents shared a point of view which David Tyack calls "administrative progressivism" (*One Best System*, pp. 182–98). Mary Herrick notes that Haley supported McAndrew's appointment (*Chicago Schools*, p. 143). George S. Counts, *School and Society in Chicago*, pp. 98–99, shares her conclusion. Haley claimed to have been suspicious of McAndrew from the beginning, although she acknowledged that people in Chicago thought that she supported him ("Autobiography," 1935, p. 585, CTF Coll., Box 34).

15. Alexander Fichlander, "Teachers' Ratings"; William McAndrew, "Rating of Teachers."

16. Counts, *School and Society*, pp. 71–81.

17. Ibid., pp. 116–23, 3–5.

18. Henry Linville to Charles Stillman, 29 Oct. 1917, Linville Coll., Box 2. Although Linville eventually opposed the Gary reforms, he was appalled when many labor unionists and parents supported the Tammany candidate for mayor in 1917 because of that politician's outspoken antipathy to the plan. Linville proposed instead that teachers and parents support the socialist candidate, Morris Hilquit. See Henry Linville to Morris Hilquit, 23 Oct. 1917, Linville Coll., Box 2.

19. Haley, "Autobiography, 1935, p. 594, CTF Coll., Box 34. For Chicago elementary-school teachers' opposition to McAndrew, see Herrick, *Chicago Schools*, pp. 146–48.

20. Herrick, *Chicago Schools*, pp. 155–57; Counts, *School and Society*, pp. 3–6.

21. William McAndrew, "Criticize in Writing," p. 437; quoted in Counts, *School and Society*, pp. 75–76.

Chapter 8

1. Wayne J. Urban, "The Effects of Ideology and Power on a Teacher Walkout."
2. Willard Waller, *The Sociology of Teaching*, chap. 5; Dan C. Lortie, *Schoolteacher*; Myron Brenton, *What's Happened to Teacher?*, chap. 2. I have attempted to illustrate the continuity between the early twentieth century and the contemporary scene in terms of issues and teachers' reactions in "Past and Present in Educational Innovation."
3. Cole, *Unionization of Teachers*, pp. 14–15, 18–21.

Bibliography

Addams, Jane. *Twenty Years at Hull House*. New York: Macmillan, 1910.

Alexander, Carter. *Some Present Aspects of the Work of Teachers' Voluntary Associations*. Teachers College, Columbia University Contributions to Education no. 36. New York: Teachers College, Columbia University, 1910.

Anderson, Olive O. "The Chicago Teachers' Federation." Master's thesis, University of Chicago, 1908.

Atlanta. Georgia State University Southern Labor Archives. Atlanta Education Association Collection.

———. Atlanta Historical Society. Atlanta Schools Collection.

———. Emory University Library Special Collections. Mary Barker Papers.

Brenton, Myron. *What's Happened to Teacher?* New York: Coward McCann, 1970.

Buchanan, Frederick S. "Unpacking of the N.E.A.: The Role of Utah's Teachers at the 1920 Convention." *Utah Historical Quarterly* 41 (1973):150–61.

Buenker, John D. *Urban Liberalism and Progressive Reform*. New York: Charles Scribner's Sons, 1973.

Callahan, Raymond E. *Education and the Cult of Efficiency*. Chicago: University of Chicago Press, 1962.

———. "The History of the Fight to Control Policy in Public Education." In *The Struggle for Power in Education*, edited by Frank W. Lutz and Joseph Azzarelli, pp. 16–34. New York: Center for Applied Research in Education, 1966.

Chicago. Chicago Historical Society. Chicago Teachers' Federation Collection.

Church, Robert L. *Education in the United States: An Interpretive History*. New York: Free Press, 1976.

Clarke, James E. "The American Federation of Teachers: Origins and History from 1870 to 1952." Ph.D. dissertation, Cornell University, 1952.

Coffman, Lotus D. *The Social Composition of the Teaching Population*. Teachers College, Columbia University Contributions to Education no. 41. New York: Teachers College, Columbia University, 1911.

Cole, Stephen. *The Unionization of Teachers: A Case Study of the UFT*. New York: Praeger Publishers, 1969.

Committee on Teachers' Salaries, Tenure, and the Cost of Living. *Teachers' Salaries and the Cost of Living*. Washington, D.C.: National Education Association, 1918.

Counts, George S. *School and Society in Chicago*. New York: Harcourt Brace, 1928.

Crabtree, J. W. *What Counted Most*. Lincoln, Nebr.: University Publishing Co., 1953.

Creel, George. "Why Chicago's Teachers Unionized." *Margaret Haley's Bulletin* 1 (1915):3–4.

Crimmins, Timothy James. "The Crystal Stair: A Study of the Effects of Class, Race, and Ethnicity on Secondary Education in Atlanta, 1872–1925." Ph.D. dissertation, Emory University, 1972.

Detroit. Wayne State University Archives of Labor and Urban Affairs. American Federation of Teachers Collection.

————. Wayne State University Archives of Labor and Urban Affairs. Henry R. Linville Collection.

Eaton, William Edward. *The American Federation of Teachers, 1916–1961: A History of the Movement*. Carbondale, Ill.: Southern Illinois University Press, 1975.

Ecke, Melvin W. *From Ivy Street to Kennedy Center: Centennial History of the Atlanta Public School System*. Atlanta, Ga.: Atlanta Board of Education, 1972.

Fahey, Sara H. "History of the Department of Classroom Teachers," in *Fourth Yearbook of the Department of Classroom Teachers*, pp. 172–83. Washington, D.C.: Department of Classroom Teachers, 1929.

Fichlander, Alexander, "Teachers' Ratings." *Journal of Education* 91 (1920):36–37.

Folger, John K., and Nam, Charles B. *Education of the American Population*. A 1960 Census Monograph. Washington, D.C.: U.S. Government Printing Office, 1967.

Gilmer, Mary Fant. "History, Activities, and Present Status of the Atlanta School Teachers' Association." Master's thesis, Emory University, 1939.

Gutman, Herbert G. *Work, Culture, and Society in Industrializing America.*. New York: Random House, Vintage Books, 1977.

Hall, G. Stanley. "The Case of the Public Schools: The Witness of the School Teacher." *Atlantic Monthly* 77 (1896):402–13.

Hammack, David C. "The Centralization of New York City's Public School System." Master's thesis, Columbia University, 1969.

Hays, Samuel P. *The Response to Industrialism: 1885–1914*. Chicago: University of Chicago Press, 1957.

Herrick, Mary J. *The Chicago Schools: A Social and Political History*. Beverly Hills, Calif.: Sage Publications, 1971.

Hewes, F. W. "The Public Schools of the United States." *Harper's Weekly* 39 (1894):1017.

Hofstadter, Richard. *The Age of Reform*. New York: Random House, Vintage Books, 1955.

Jones, L. H. "The Politician and the Public Schools." *Atlantic Monthly* 77 (1896):810–22.

Karson, Marc. *American Labor Unions and Politics, 1900–1918*. Carbondale, Ill.: Southern Illinois University Press, 1957.

Katz, Michael B. *Class, Bureaucracy and Schools: The Illusion of Educational Change in America*. New York: Praeger Publishers, 1971.

————. *The Irony of Early School Reform: Educational Innovation in Mid-Nineteenth Century Massachusetts*. Cambridge, Mass.: Harvard University Press, 1968.

Kraditor, Aileen. *The Ideas of the Woman Suffrage Movement 1880–1920*. Garden City, N.Y.: Doubleday, Anchor Books, 1971.

Krug, Edward A. *The Shaping of the American High School, 1890–1920.* New York: Harper and Row, 1964.

Lieberman, Myron P. *Education as a Profession.* Englewood Cliffs, N.J.: Prentice-Hall, 1957.

Lortie, Dan C. *Schoolteacher: A Sociological Study.* Chicago: University of Chicago Press, 1975.

Lorwin, Lewis L. *The American Federation of Labor: History, Policies, and Prospects.* Washington, D.C.: The Brookings Institution, 1933.

McAndrew, William. "The Control of the Teacher's Job." *American Teacher* 5 (1916):103–5.

———. "Criticize in Writing." *Journal of Education* 83 (1916):43.

———. "Rating of Teachers." *Journal of Education* 91 (1920):243.

McManis, John T. *Ella Flagg Young and a Half Century of the Chicago Public Schools.* Chicago: A. C. McClurg, 1916.

Mears, Louise W. *The Life and Times of a Midwest Educator: Carroll Gardner Pearse.* Lincoln, Nebr.: State Journal Printing Company, 1944.

Merriam, Charles E. *Chicago: A More Intimate View of Urban Politics.* New York: Macmillan, 1920.

Morison, Samuel Eliot. "A Memoir and Estimate of Albert Bushnell Hart." *Proceedings of the Massachusetts Historical Society* 78 (1965):28–52.

National Education Association Committee on Salaries, Tenure, and Pensions. "A Comparative Study of the Salaries of Teachers and School Officers." United States Bureau of Education, Bulletin no. 31 (1915).

———. "State Pension Systems for Public School Teachers." United States Bureau of Education, Bulletin no. 14 (1916).

———. "The Tangible Rewards of Teaching." United States Bureau of Education, Bulletin no. 16 (1914).

Nelson, Daniel. *Managers and Workers: Origins of the New Factory System in the United States 1880–1920.* Madison, Wis.: University of Wisconsin Press, 1975.

Newell, Barbara W. *Chicago and the Labor Movement.* Urbana, Ill.: University of Illinois Press, 1961.

Newman, Joseph W. "A History of the Atlanta Public School Teachers' Association, Local 89 of the American Federation of Teachers, 1919–1956." Ph.D. dissertation, Georgia State University, 1978.

Pearse, Robert F. "Studies in White Collar Unionism." Ph.D. dissertation, University of Chicago, 1950.

Preston, Howard L. *Automobile Age Atlanta: The Making of A Southern Metropolis, 1900–1935.* Athens, Ga.: University of Georgia Press, 1979.

Racine, Philip Noel. "Atlanta's Schools: A History of the Public School System 1869–1955." Ph.D. dissertation, Emory University, 1969.

Ravitch, Diane. *The Great School Wars: New York City, 1805–1973.* New York: Basic Books. 1974.

Reid, Robert L. "The Professionalization of Public School Teachers: The Chicago Experience, 1895–1920." Ph.D. dissertation, Northwestern University, 1968.

Report of a Committee of the National Education Association on Teachers' Salaries and the Cost of Living. Ann Arbor, Mich.: National Education Association, 1913.

Report of the Education Commission of the City of Chicago. Chicago: R. R. Donnelly and Sons, 1899.

Reports of the Elementary Teachers' General Council. 1921–1924. Chicago, Illinois.

Rice, Joseph M. "The Public School System of New York City." *Forum* 14 (1893):616–30.

Riis, Jacob. "The Children of the Poor." In *Jacob Riis Revisited*, edited by Francesco Cordasco, pp. 125–298. New York: Doubleday, Anchor Books, 1968.

Schmid, Ralph D. "A Study of the Organizational Structure of the National Education Association, 1884–1921." Ph.D. dissertation, Washington University, 1963.

Smith, Joan K. *Ella Flagg Young: Portrait of A Leader*. Ames, Iowa: Educational Studies Press, 1980.

————. "Progressivism and the Teacher Union Movement." *Educational Studies* 7 (1976):44–61.

Spaulding, Frank E. *School Superintendent in Action in Five Cities*. Rindge, N.H.: Richard R. Smith, 1955.

Spero, Sterling D. *Government as Employer*. New York: Remsen Press, 1948.

Strachan, Grace. *Equal Pay for Equal Work*. New York: B. F. Buck, 1910.

Taft, Philip. *The A.F. of L. in the Time of Gompers*. New York: Harper & Brothers, 1957.

————. *United They Teach: The Story of the United Federation of Teachers*. Los Angeles: Nash Publishing, 1974.

Thelen, David. *Robert M. LaFollette and the Insurgent Spirit*. Boston: Little Brown, 1976.

Tyack, David B. *The One Best System: A History of American Urban Education, 1890–1940*. Cambridge, Mass.: Harvard University Press, 1974.

Urban, Wayne J. "The Effects of Ideology and Power on a Teacher Walkout: Florida, 1968." *Journal of Collective Negotiations in the Public Sector* 3 (1974):133–46.

————. "Organized Teachers and Educational Reform during the Progressive Era: 1890–1920." *History of Education Quarterly* 16 (1976):35–52.

————. "The Past and the Present in Educational Innovation: Scientific Management and Competency Based Education." *Foundational Studies* 6 (1977):5–17.

————. "Progressive Education in the Urban South: The Reform of the Atlanta Schools, 1914–1918." In *The Age of Urban Reform: New Perspectives on the Progressive Era*, edited by Michael Ebner and Eugene Tobin, pp. 131–41. Port Washington, N.Y.: Kennikat, 1977.

Van Tine, Warren R. *The Making of the Labor Bureaucrat*. Amherst, Mass.: University of Massachusetts Press, 1973.

Viggers, Christine Anne. "The Importance of the Women Teacher's Organization in the Equal Pay for Teachers Controversy." Master's thesis, University of Oregon, 1973.

Waller, Willard. *The Sociology of Teaching*. New York: John Wiley, 1932.

Wattenberg, William W. *On the Educational Front: The Reactions of Teachers Associations in New York and Chicago*. New York: Pierre Q. Pasquer, 1936.

Wesley, Edgar B. *NEA: The First Hundred Years*. New York: Harper & Brothers, 1957.

Woodward, C. Vann. *Origins of the New South, 1877–1913*. Baton Rouge, La.: Louisiana State University Press, 1951.

Yellowitz, Irwin. *Labor and the Progressive Movement in New York State, 1897–1916*. Ithaca, N.Y.: Cornell University Press, 1965.

Zitron, Celia Lewis. *The New York City Teachers Union 1916–1964: A Story of Educational and Social Commitment*. New York: Humanities Press, 1968.

Index

Wayne J. Urban was educated at John Carroll University (B.S.S., 1963) and Ohio State University (M.A., 1965; Ph.D., 1968), and has taught at several institutions, including the universities of Florida and South Florida, Kent State University, the University of Alabama in Birmingham, and the University of Wisconsin, Madison. He is currently professor and chairman, Department of Educational Foundations, Georgia State University.

Professor Urban has served as president of the History of Education Society and has been a member of the editorial boards of the *History of Education Quarterly* and *Educational Studies*; he is now editor of the latter journal. He has previously published articles and reviews in the *History of Education Quarterly*, the *Review of Education*, and the *Harvard Educational Review*, and is coauthor (with Don T. Martin and others) of *Accountability in American Education: A Critique* (1976).

The manuscript was edited by Sherwyn T. Carr. The book was designed by Mary Primeau.

The typeface for the text is Mergenthaler's VIP Bookman, based on a design by Alexander Phemister about 1860. The display face is Bookman. The book is printed on 60 lb. Booktext natural textpaper and bound in Permalin Buckram cloth over binder's boards.

Manufactured in the United States of America.